Positive Parenting for Toddlers

The Ultimate Guide to Calm Tantrums and Build a Strong, Loving Bond with Your Toddler

Table of Contents

Introduction

Parenting a toddler can be an uphill battle. They are confused about what it means to exist in the world, and you are unsure how to guide them. There are thousands of parenting approaches, all claiming to be the golden goose that can transform a Tasmanian devil into a well-behaved angel. However, the positive parenting method is backed by the latest psychological research and has repeatedly proven its effectiveness.

Positive parenting is the idea that children should be taught what to do instead of what not to do. This sounds intuitive on its face, but it's surprising how many actions parents inadvertently take that undermine this principle. This parenting framework centers on relationship, connection, and communication as the pillars of uplifting a well-developed child.

Every aspect of your child's being is covered, from emotional health to social skills. Positive parenting co-creates an environment where your child's needs and desires are acknowledged while their autonomy is fostered. Applying this parenting method has endless benefits that will help your child grow into a socially and psychologically equipped adult.

This comprehensive guide teaches you how to use positive parenting to raise well-behaved, emotionally intelligent, and independent children. The text stands out because it gives you the theory and psychological background to fully understand the framework while providing practical ways to implement it.

This book is the bridge of understanding between you and your toddler. You will learn how to communicate at their level and how to craft your words and actions to be maximally impactful. The toddler years can be intimidating, but this text is the steady ship that navigates the patchy waters.

Your child is in the transitionary stage between an infant and an adolescent. These integral years will shape their personality and psyche for the rest of their lives. Positive parenting mindfully maneuvers this sensitive time to give your child every social, psychological, and emotional advantage.

The turbulence of raising a toddler can be frustrating. It takes patience and commitment. The difficulty is amplified when you are unsure of which direction to take. The techniques explored in this text are ways to ease the burden by creating a relationship of collaboration with your toddler. Instead of standing before your child as the bullying dictator, you promote a relationship of trust and motivation.

There is no magic potion to transform your child into a well-behaved saint. The methods in this book take time and commitment. Positive parenting is not about quick fixes; it focuses on the daily repetitions and habitual lessons you facilitate in your relationship with your child. By immersing yourself in these lessons, you reveal a transformative approach to parenting that radically benefits you and your child.

Chapter 1: Getting to Know Your Toddler

Before you learn how to parent your toddler, it's a good idea to get to know them a little better. This chapter provides comprehensive cognitive, physical, emotional, and social milestones toddlers reach during their development to help you familiarize yourself with their needs at this crucial stage. This will lay the foundation for a deeper understanding of your child's needs so you can help them navigate life and have a happy and balanced childhood.

Before you can parent effectively, you need to get to know your toddler.[1]

Toddler Stages

The toddler stage, the period between ages one and three, is one of the most transformative phases of a child's life. During this period, your child will reach several developmental milestones and learn many new skills that allow them to become independent. In the span of these three years, your child goes from being a baby barely able to take a few steps or communicate to a curious toddler who runs and forms full sentences.

Typical toddler milestones are based on what most toddlers can do at a certain stage, like moving, playing, socializing, learning, etc. Toddlerhood is crucial because 80% of your child's brain functions, including language, memory, reasoning, and thinking skills, are developed by age three. Most of what your child learns comes from imitating you, other adults, and older children in their lives, so parenting plays a fundamental role in their development at this stage.

Seeing your toddler discover their independence and spread their wings is a sight to behold and cherish. At the same time, their need to establish autonomy will lead them to defiant behavior, which makes helping them explore the world safely all the more challenging.

Below are the detailed developmental milestones for toddlers broken down into age groups and categories.

12-18 Months

Socio-Emotional Milestones

- handing objects to others (they consider this play)
- can have minor temper tantrums
- can be afraid of strangers (not all toddlers are)
- can show affection to familiar people like parents/caregivers and close family members
- know how to play simple pretend, like feeding their doll or moving a car
- may cling to caregivers in new situations
- points to show you when they see something interesting, like an animal walking by
- they start to explore alone, but still, caregivers stay close to them
- start imitating others

Language and Communication Milestones

- can clearly say several single words, including "yes" and "no"
- indicate when they do not want something by shaking their head
- can point to show you something they want
- know how to wave "bye-bye"
- begin to show defiance

Cognitive Milestones

- know what ordinary objects are for – like spoons, brushes, and phones
- can point to objects or persons to get people's attention
- start showing deeper interest in toys and how to play with them
- can point to their body parts
- start scribbling on their own
- can understand simple one-step instructions (without any gestures) – for example, they will sit if you say "sit down"
- they are aware of themselves and their surroundings and explore them even more
- they are curious about meeting new people
- they can recognize themselves in a mirror

Physical Development and Movement Milestones

- start walking independently
- may walk up steps (sometimes the walking will be a mixture of crawling, running, and actual walking)
- can pull toys after themselves while walking
- can help undress themselves
- can eat with a spoon and drink from a cup independently

18-24 Months

Socio-Emotional Milestones

- regularly imitate others, especially adults and older children
- get excited when encountering other children
- show increased independence
- want to do what they have been told not to
- play mainly beside other children but begin to include them in certain games

Language and Communication Milestones

- point to objects or pictures when named
- know and recognize the names of familiar people
- can name most of their body parts
- say and use two- to four-word sentences
- can follow simple instructions (with gestures)
- may repeat words they overhear in conversation
- can point to objects and animals in a book

Cognitive Milestones

- can find objects even when they are hidden (for example, under a cover)
- start sorting colors and shapes
- can complete slightly longer sentences
- recognize and recite rhymes from familiar books
- capable of playing easy-to-follow games that are make-believe
- has the ability to stack blocks
- will possibly begin having a more dominant hand
- has the ability to follow instructions that include 2 steps
- capable of identifying images in a picture book, like dogs, birds, cats, etc.

Physical Development and Movement Milestones

- can stand on their tiptoes unassisted
- can kick a ball
- start running
- can climb onto and down from furniture unassisted
- can walk up and down stairs holding on to the railing or another person's hand

At this stage, the toddler's desire to be independent becomes the strongest, so this is when parents experience the most challenges. Yet observing how your child experiences their world and develops their understanding of themselves and others can be an exciting time. You'll see them explore, think, learn, and experience many changes as they make sense of their surroundings. By being ever cautious, they'll observe and imitate you and other older relatives (including siblings and cousins) as well as playmates. Your child also starts expressing emotions but doesn't yet understand or control them; hence, why the intense feelings lead to temper tantrums.

2-3 Years

Socio-Emotional Milestones

- copying kids that are older and adults as well
- being able to show emotions towards friends without being told to
- can wait for their turn in a game
- has the ability to show empathy or worry if a friend cries.
- grasps the concepts of ownership – his, hers, or mine
- displays varying emotions
- can differentiate between the mother and father
- will show discomfort when the routine is changed
- is able to get dressed and undressed on their own

Language and Communication Milestones:

- follow instructions with two or three steps
- can name the most familiar things
- understand words like "in," "on," and "under"
- say first name, age, and sex
- name a friend
- say words like "I," "me," "we," and "you," and some plurals (cars, dogs, cats)
- talk well enough for strangers to understand most of the time
- carry on a conversation using two to three sentences

Cognitive Milestones

- has the ability to operate toys that have moving parts, toys, and buttons
- enjoys creating their own world while playing with animals, people, and toys
- can tackle simple 3 or 4-piece puzzles
- can duplicate a shape such as a circle
- has the ability to handle a book and turn the pages
- can stack towers that consist of 6 blocks or more
- has the ability to unscrew and screw lids and also use door handles

Physical Development and Movement Milestones

- climb well
- run easily
- pedal a tricycle (a three-wheel bike)
- walk up and down stairs, one foot on each step

The Importance of Toddlerhood

Between ages one and two, the number of connections in a toddler's neurons doubles. This leads to a rapid spurt in the development of multiple areas of the brain, including the learning region, enabling toddlers to learn twice as fast as they did before. They also learn much faster than adults because adults already have fewer neurons. For the same reasons, toddlerhood is critical in shaping a child's foundational skills and behaviors. By encouraging them to explore and learn (focusing on breadth instead of depth), modeling emotional intelligence, and having them learn at their own pace as toddlers, you can lay the foundation for further growth and development.

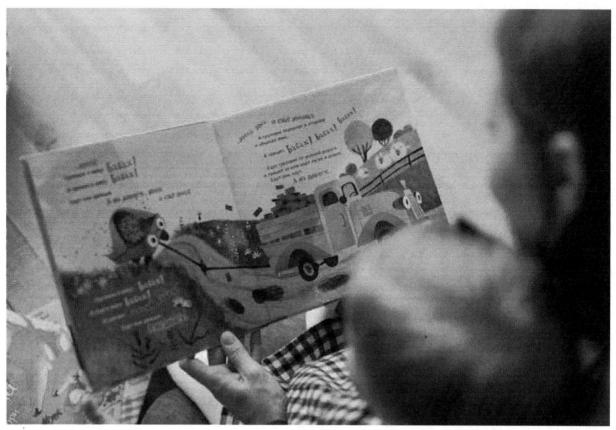
Toddlers learn especially fast if they can focus on exploring and satisfying their curiosity.[2]

Toddlers learn especially fast if they can focus on exploring and satisfying their curiosity. They don't care about performance, but they'll be happy to try new activities because they always want to learn something new. During this stage, they'll also familiarize themselves with the concept of mistakes, and by modeling caregivers, they can understand that making mistakes is a normal part of life.

During this intense learning period, toddlers start developing a growth mindset, which, unlike adults, comes naturally to small children. They want to explore their skills and discover new abilities. Moreover, each toddler has a unique identity and way of learning that should be respected. They don't understand universal labels yet (like smart), so using these will only confuse them.

Children who see the love of learning in caregivers will be even more enthusiastic about their learning journey. When trying out something new yourself, older toddlers will be happy to join you if you ask them. It's a wonderful opportunity for them to observe how you relate to the world and start emulating this as a new skill.

Toddlers like to be exposed to a broad range of activities, like dancing, reading, creating art, learning language skills, trying a new game that requires movement, etc. This lays the foundation for many skills they'll make use of later in life. Their abstract and creative thinking develops further by learning to draw from multiple areas.

They naturally focus on breadth, not depth, so they often get bored with an activity (especially if there is something new they can try). This is normal and only contributes to them becoming well-rounded children and adults. They have plenty of time to deepen their skills later, and by sampling the different skills, they'll have a wider variety to choose from.

Emotional intelligence is a critical skill children learn from their relationships with caregivers and others in their lives. By observing others, your toddler acquires interpersonal skills like empathy and kindness. They also learn to work with others and take initiative when they want to achieve something. They start by observing how you acknowledge their feelings. Hearing you label them and your emotions and connecting them to their original source is one of the most decisive milestones in a toddler's socio-emotional development. It's when they learn to acknowledge their feelings, which is the first step in learning to control them. Remember, as they enter toddlerhood, your child starts experiencing plenty of new emotions. However, they can't control them or where they come from. By learning that they feel sad because they didn't get to have their favorite treat, for example, they start making sense of their feelings. Once they learn about their own emotions, they'll also be curious about other people's emotions. For example, they'll want to know why other people are sad, too, and may even start making the connection between their feelings and others' emotions in certain situations.

Toddlerhood is also crucial for learning teamwork. Most children are happy to be included in chores, which is a great way for them to learn how to be helpful to others.

Unique Temperament

Unique temperament is your toddler's individual way of making sense of and responding to the world around them. It has a vast influence on your child's behavior, so respecting and appreciating their unique learning qualities is paramount for their health and happiness. By receiving acceptance of their individual needs, skills, abilities, and learning styles, children can develop healthy coping skills when facing challenges. At the end of toddlerhood, most children enter into a new social community – a new environment where the number of challenges they face will increase exponentially. Parenting children in a way they know that their different qualities, flaws, and personalities are accepted helps them maximize their strengths and work on their weaknesses. This is especially crucial for parents of multiple children. Children can have different needs even during the same stage of their lives, so a parenting technique that works for an older sibling may not work for your toddler. It's also not a good idea to compare children because this will only make them notice and magnify their flaws but not their talents.

Your child's unique temperament shines through the way they:

- React to situations that evoke strong emotions, like when they can't get what they want or when they are excited about getting something. Some children react stronger than others.

- Regulate themselves, including their emotions. Some children are better at controlling and expressing their emotions at an early age. Regulations also show how good they are at paying attention and being persistent when wanting something.

- Socialize when meeting new people. Some children are comfortable right away in a new community, while others take more time to warm up.

- Adapt to changes in their regular environment or new situations. Not every child will be able to adapt right away, and some need more help adjusting.

- Require physical activity as some children need exercise. They can get restless and fidgety otherwise, which can also affect their sleep. Others don't need as much activity.

- Adopt rhythmic or regular behaviors, including sleeping, eating, and going to the bathroom. Although they need consistency, some children struggle with getting into a regular pattern for basic functions.

- Approach and withdraw from situations where they receive a new stimulus or have a new experience. Some children are more hesitant to approach these, while others are bolder.

- Display intensity when responding to new situations, whether these are negative or positive. Some toddlers have a more intense reaction, even to the smallest excitement.

- Children who are in a good mood most of the time often use positive words and behaviors, while those in a perpetually bad mood are characterized by negative speech and behavior.

- Focus on a single task without getting distracted by something or someone. Some children can be distracted by the smallest sounds and sights and leave the task unfinished, while others can focus longer.

- Indicate their sensory threshold or how much stimulation they need to respond to a stimulus. Most toddlers need a small amount of stimulation, but in some cases, they can require more.

All these indicators of temperament are innate, meaning your child was born with them. You can't change their temperament, so it's crucial to adapt your parenting style to it. Temperament indicators also explain why siblings can have different dispositions. For example, one sibling might be less reactive than the other, or one is more sociable than the other. By nurturing each child's development through temperament-focused parenting, you can help them grow the strongest parts of their disposition.

Adapting your parenting style to each child's temperament can also help you understand what they're going through in different situations. You'll be able to see whether they are struggling with something because of their temperament, and you can help them overcome their difficulties.

Parenting more reactive children requires a different approach than parenting less reactive children. For example, reactive children often respond loudly and energetically to stimuli, so they need to learn *calmer responses*. Less reactive children are calmer but may find it difficult to stand up for themselves, which is something you can work on together to build their confidence. More reactive children also require more physical activity throughout the day than their less reactive peers, so this should also be incorporated into their parenting.

Likewise, parenting children who are better at self-regulation and those who have poor self-regulation skills will differ. Children with good self-regulation skills will be persistent and rarely get frustrated when dealing with a difficult task. However, they can be perfectionists and need to learn that mistakes are normal. On the other hand, less self-regulated children can have difficulty paying attention and easily give up on difficult tasks – unless they are expecting a reward at the end. They're very creative, so focusing on artful activities may be a better approach to parenting.

While sociable toddlers love playdates, they should also learn how to occupy themselves to avoid becoming overly reliant on others. Less sociable children often need to work on making friends, and they feel uncomfortable in larger groups. Both qualities should be considered during parenting.

While sociable toddlers love playdates, they should also learn how to occupy themselves to avoid becoming overly reliant on others.[3]

Adoptable children can cope with new situations and unexpected changes, even when it comes to switching who they spend time with. Parenting them will be different than raising less adoptable children, who prefer sticking to routines. They may not enjoy surprises, let alone facing transitions.

Another crucial factor to consider is your own temperament. Parents love to discover parts of their personality in their children because they feel this will make it easier to understand their toddlers. For example, if you're less adaptable, you may find it easier to parent a child who prefers strict routines. However, you may have to face the possibility that your child's (or children's) disposition will be different from yours. They might dislike routines just as much as you like them. While this can make parenting more challenging, it's also a great opportunity to learn about your child's temperament.

One of the lessons you can learn by observing your child's disposition is that parts of their behavior are beyond their control. They don't act in a way you wouldn't expect of them just to defy you. They do it because their temperament drives them to do it. Understanding this can relieve some of the stress you feel, enabling you to become more patient and find a different approach to parenting. In turn, your child will feel less pressure, and they will be able to focus on learning new skills that improve their temperament.

Regardless of a toddler's unique temperament, parenting can foster healthy development. It's a question of finding the right approach and grabbing teachable moments when you can put it into practice. Remember, whenever they're near you, your toddler will look up to you. However, if you react to specific situations, they'll watch you and learn from your reaction. Children learn more from actions, so real-life situations will always be more helpful teaching aids than books and lessons. This is especially true for toddlers who, while learning fast, don't know how to put things into context. For instance, a reactive toddler may not understand when you tell them that they have to use less angry and loud words, but they'll understand when you remain calm when the water boils over on the stove instead of getting upset.

If your toddler has a more challenging temperament, don't worry. With appropriate parenting, you can help them learn to alter their behaviors. For instance, by teaching a child with a more intense ratio to respond more calmly, their intensity can turn to zeal and enthusiasm with age.

Children's temperaments naturally change with age. As they mature, toddlers can understand more and more how their behavior in different situations affects them and their environment. They also begin to grasp that their experiences can impact their emotions and actions. For example, an easily distracted child can learn that they can enjoy group activities (sports, games, etc.) more if they pay attention.

The Joy of Raising Toddlers

Parenting toddlers may not be the easiest job in the world, but as the following stories indicate, understanding and connecting with a growing and curious child brings tremendous joy and happiness.

"When my daughter was a baby, I used to think of changing their diaper as one more task to get done. However, since she began walking and exploring the world, I found it harder and harder to get in close and connect with her. I love observing my daughter as she wanders around curiously, picks up objects, and tries to make sense of her surroundings, but I miss some of the close moments we had before she became an independent toddler. So, now I use little moments like diaper change to bond with her. I sing her silly songs and look her into her eyes while I change her. This distracts her and makes it a happy time instead of making her upset for preventing her from whatever exploration she was doing when I picked her up. She sings along by making funny sounds, imitating me, and we both have a great time." – Tamara

"Life with a toddler is hectic, but it can be vastly entertaining. I could be weighted down with preoccupations, but when my 10-month-old son suddenly turns to me and says "Hi" smilingly, I can't help but return the smile, and soon we're both giggling. We usually play on the floor because he can get so excited during play that he would fall from any height. I often marvel at how he can find so much joy in little things. The other day, we were outside, and he was sitting on the top of a leaf pile, excitedly pulling out the differently-colored leaves from under him. I just stood and soaked up the world through his eyes, so happy that I could be beside him and he could show me everything he wanted." – Esther

"One of the reasons I love being a mom to a toddler is the look in their eyes when they figure something out. My child is very tenacious, and they can spend a lot of time trying to understand how something works. I love seeing how much their eyes light up when they figure it out. I also love how happy my child is when they discover something new, for example, a new skill. For example, I love singing made-up songs, and one day, I heard my almost three-year-old do the same out of the blue. They were so happy when they discovered they could do it and came to sing me the song they'd just "created." I love that I'm able to shape their mind and share something so unique with them." – Amanda

"I love being playful, so having children was a wonderful opportunity to revisit the magic of childhood. Now that I have two toddlers (an 18-month-old and a two-and-a-half-year-old), I'm so happy that I can share with them the joy of discovering how to do things on their own. I love being there to

encourage them and receive the hugs of happiness when they get it right. They're both still discovering new words, too, which is also fun. Our house is full of giggles and laughter most of the time because I see how much they can learn when having fun. While parenting them also helped me to become more patient, I truly appreciate all the beautiful moments I have with my family." - Ben

"Parenting a toddler can be a humbling experience. It taught me to become more loving and patient and not to take everything seriously. I have a stressful job, so this was a good thing. When I am happy to have finished a long day at work, I'm greeted by a curious child who laughs at everything, including when they inform me that I have to change their diaper. They are becoming more and more independent every day, which brings on challenges like them not wanting to eat the food we prepare for them. When they do and want more, we consider that a win. I learned that liking/disliking food is just part of my child's personality, and I like how it shines through, even though this leads to a not-so-infrequent standstill at dinner. I think it is a blessing to see them grow and spread their independence, and it's up to us parents to help them on this wonderful journey." - Angel

Chapter 2: Becoming a Positive Parent

Parenting is not merely a series of tasks to be completed but a journey of self-discovery and growth. Your upbringing, experiences, and cultural influences will shape how you parent your toddler. To become a positive parent, you first need to recognize that not all of your inherited beliefs and patterns will create a nurturing environment for your little angel. Self-reflection is the right practice and can be your way to effective parenting. It allows you to tap into your deeply ingrained beliefs and attitudes, understand their origins, and evaluate whether they align with the goals of raising happy, resilient, and confident toddlers.

Take a moment to ponder the parenting practices you experienced as a child.'

Take a moment to ponder the parenting practices you experienced as a child. How do these experiences influence the way you interact with your toddler? Are there any beliefs or attitudes you hold about parenting that may be limiting or outdated? How do you respond to challenging situations with your toddler? Are these responses driven by conscious choices or automatic reactions?

You may find that some of your beliefs and behaviors work great for your toddler's development, while others must be examined and revamped if necessary. It's okay to challenge conventional wisdom and embrace new approaches that resonate with your values and aspirations as a parent.

Self-reflection paves the way for a more conscious and intentional parenting journey. You become better equipped to respond to your toddler's needs with empathy, patience, and understanding. Above all, you create a loving and supportive environment where your toddler can thrive and flourish.

Reflective Prompts to Use

- When faced with challenging behavior from your toddler, pause and ask yourself what underlying need or emotion might be driving this behavior and how you can address this need with empathy and understanding.

- As a parent, when you encounter a behavior from your toddler that pushes your buttons, take a moment before reacting. Instead of reacting impulsively, consider what might be causing your child to act this way. Is it a need for attention or perhaps frustration due to not being understood? When you can identify the root cause of the behavior, you respond with empathy and find constructive ways to meet your toddler's needs.

- You can also reflect on your childhood experiences. Question yourself whether there are any patterns or behaviors from your past that you find yourself repeating in your parenting approach. How do these patterns impact your interactions with your toddler?

- Reflect on how these patterns influence your interactions with your toddler and whether they align with the parent you aspire to be.

- Take a moment to evaluate the expectations you hold for your toddler's behavior. Are they realistic, given your child's age and stage of development? Reflect on how these expectations shape your reactions to your toddler's actions. Unrealistic expectations will only lead to frustration and disappointment, whereas setting developmentally appropriate goals allows for more understanding and patience.

- Explore your emotional responses to parenting. What coping strategies do you employ when you feel overwhelmed, frustrated, or anxious? Consider healthier ways to manage stress and regulate your emotions, like deep breathing, mindfulness, or seeking support from a partner or friend.

- Pay attention to the language you use when interacting with your toddler. Is it positive and encouraging, or does it lean toward criticism and negativity? Reflect on how your words and tone impact your child's self-esteem and behavior. Aim to communicate in a way that promotes cooperation, mutual respect, and a positive parent-child relationship.

- Consider the values and beliefs you want to instill in your toddler as they grow. Reflect on whether your current parenting practices fall in line with these values. Are there opportunities to model these values through your actions and interactions with your child?

- Take a moment to define what it means to be a good parent. Is it about promoting independence, nurturing emotional intelligence, or something else? Reflect on how these expectations shape your parenting decisions and interactions with your toddler. Remember that there are no universal rules for being a good parent, and it's okay to adjust your expectations based on your unique circumstances and values.

As you practice these reflective prompts to open your mind, remember that adjusting your expectations, thoughts, and reactions to parenting challenges can make a huge difference. Parenthood is undoubtedly a path full of challenges, frustrations, and moments of exhaustion. However, how you perceive and respond to these challenges can profoundly impact your parenting experience and the well-being of your cute shining star.

Reflecting on your beliefs, attitudes, and behaviors is indeed a proactive step toward becoming a calmer and more positive parent. It's about shifting your perspective from seeing struggles as obstacles to viewing them as opportunities for growth and learning for you and your child.

Adjusting your thoughts and feelings about parenting struggles creates space for greater patience, understanding, and resilience. Instead of feeling overwhelmed by every hiccup and tantrum, you can approach these moments calmly and confidently.

Furthermore, keeping a positive attitude toward every task will not only keep your nerves calm but also leave a positive impact on your toddler's mind. They will slowly recognize which behaviors are acceptable and develop emotional intelligence. With each adjustment, you pave the way for a brighter and more fulfilling parenting experience filled with moments of joy, connection, and growth.

Taking a Proactive Approach

Parenthood is an ongoing journey that requires you to care for your toddler and support them through their phases of development. However, there will be times when everything feels overwhelming. This is when taking on a proactive parenting approach will be beneficial.

It involves anticipating challenges, setting clear intentions, and consciously choosing responses to various situations. Instead of merely reacting to your child's behaviors at the moment, you take proactive steps to create a supportive environment that promotes their growth and development at all levels.

Here is how a proactive approach enhances the overall parenting experience and makes it more fruitful:

Builds Stronger Connections

Approaching parenting proactively lays the foundation for building strong connections with your child based on trust, empathy, and caring actions. The meaningful interactions you make and the quality time you spend together deepen your bond and create lasting memories. For example, before leaving for the park, involve your toddler in simple preparations, like putting on their shoes or choosing a favorite toy to bring along. Keep your explanations short and simple by using gestures and simple language they can understand. Furthermore, engage in simple activities together, like pushing them on the swing, exploring the sandbox, or playing peek-a-boo behind trees. Follow their lead and let them dictate the pace of the outing.

Promotes Problem-Solving

With proactive parenting, you can encourage your toddler to develop resilience and problem-solving skills from an early age. Encouraging them to face challenges with optimism and perseverance builds the confidence and resilience needed to navigate different challenges. Say your toddler is trying to fit a puzzle piece into a puzzle but is struggling to find the right spot. Instead of solving the puzzle for them or becoming frustrated, you can take a proactive approach:

- Praise your toddler for trying to solve it.
- Keep them motivated with positive reinforcement.
- Guide their hand toward the right spot without solving it for them.
- Cheer enthusiastically when they fit the piece correctly.
- Remind them that mistakes are part of learning.
- Urge them to keep trying and not give up easily.

Promotes Positive Behavior

Adopting a proactive approach allows you to focus on reinforcing positive behavior rather than reacting to negative ones. Praise and acknowledge your child's efforts and achievements, which encourages them to continue making positive choices and contributions. For example, if you want to encourage your toddler to eat vegetables, praise them when they try a new vegetable by saying something like, "Great job trying the broccoli." Furthermore, when they have finished the meal, give them a treat like a sticker or candy for encouragement.

Proactive parenting focuses on creating a supportive environment where your child feels safe, valued, and respected. By consistently providing guidance and offering unconditional love, you lay the foundation for their well-being and success. Remember that parenthood is a journey filled with ups and downs, and by approaching it with intentionality and positivity, you can create a loving and supportive environment where both you and your child can flourish.

Tips to Shift Your Mindset

For Parents-to-Be

- To prepare for parenthood, take parenting classes, read books, and seek advice from trusted sources. Knowledge can help you become more confident and prepared.
- Discuss your parenting values, beliefs, and expectations with your partner to ensure you're on the same page and can effectively support each other.
- Prioritize your physical, emotional, and mental well-being before your baby arrives. Establish healthy habits, seek support when needed, and make time for activities that bring you joy and relaxation.
- Surround yourself with supportive friends, family members, and fellow parents who can offer guidance, encouragement, and assistance when needed.

To prepare for parenthood, take parenting classes, read books, and seek advice from trusted sources.[5]

Parenthood is unpredictable, and plans may need to change at a moment's notice. Always stay flexible and adaptable to navigate the challenges and joys of parenting with grace.

For Parents of Toddlers

- Prioritize building a strong emotional connection with your toddler through quality time, affection, and giving attention. A secure attachment lays the foundation for positive parent-child relationships.

- Establish age-appropriate expectations for your toddler. This helps your child understand what is expected of them.

- Focus on teaching and guiding your toddler through positive discipline techniques, such as praising them for good behavior. Avoid punitive measures that may harm the parent-child relationship.

- Support your toddler's growing independence by allowing them to make age-appropriate choices, like making them choose their meal or a toy they like from the toy store. This practice promotes confidence and self-esteem.

- Be a role model for your toddler by demonstrating kindness, patience, and empathy in your interactions with others. Toddlers learn by observing, so strive to portray the values and behaviors you want to instill in your child.

During this time, don't forget to prioritize your self-care as a parent. Take some time out for relaxation, hobbies, and social connections. When you are well-rested and emotionally nourished, you can better address your toddler's needs.

Here are some success stories, real-life examples, and science-backed information that will highlight the outcomes positive parenting brings:

The Power of Consistency

In parenting, consistency is a key practice that stands out above all. It's like a steady beat that guides the rhythm of parent-child interactions, creating trust, security, and resilience along the way. Consistency lays the foundation for trust in the parent-toddler relationship. When toddlers know what to expect from their caregivers, they feel secure and confident in their environment. From bedtime routines to disciplinary measures, consistent parenting signals reliability and stability, creating safety and belonging in the toddler's world.

Giving your toddler the feeling of being consistently around, responding to their cues, and validating their feelings creates an environment where they feel understood. This emotional security can become a springboard for healthy social and emotional development, allowing them to explore the world confidently.

Furthermore, supportive parenting builds a strong foundation of self-esteem and confidence in toddlers. Consistent praise and encouragement can instill a sense of worth and value in your toddler. This positive reinforcement fuels their motivation and resilience, making them ready to face challenges with courage and determination.

This parenting approach creates memories that toddlers carry throughout their lives. From the everyday moments of connection to the milestones and celebrations, these shared experiences weave a secure cocoon of love, trust, and belonging that shapes the parent-child bond for years to come.

Success Story

Anna was the mother of a two-year-old named Jill. Although Jill was an active toddler with a good diet, she often threw tantrums and showed stubborn behavior. Instead of resorting to traditional disciplinary methods, Anna decided to practice positive parenting techniques. Anna recognized that her daughter's tantrums were a normal part of her development and a way of expressing her emotions. Instead of reacting with frustration, Anna approached her daughter's tantrums with empathy and understanding, acknowledging her feelings and validating her emotions.

She remained calm and composed during her daughter's tantrums, providing a soothing presence and comfort when needed. She avoided getting into power struggles and focused on maintaining a peaceful environment. Instead of trying to reason with her daughter during a tantrum, Anna used distraction and redirection techniques to help her daughter calm down. She offered her daughter a toy or engaged her in a different activity to shift her focus away from the source of frustration.

Besides this, Anna praised her daughter's efforts when she became calm. With simple gestures, facial expressions, and simple sentences, she communicated calmly to let Jill know what behavior was acceptable and what behavior was not.

Furthermore, Anna made sure to spend quality time with her daughter outside of tantrum situations, engaging in activities they both enjoyed in order to develop a solid bond. As a result of Anna's use of positive parenting techniques, her daughter's tantrums decreased in frequency and intensity, and their relationship grew stronger.

Examples

Improved Behavior

Positive parenting techniques like praise, encouragement, and positive reinforcement lead to improved behavior. For example, when you consistently acknowledge and reward your toddler's positive actions, like sharing toys or finishing meals, it reinforces those behaviors and motivates your toddler to continue behaving in a similar manner.

Enhanced Self-Esteem

Positive parenting increases self-worth and confidence in your toddler. When you give them unconditional love, support, and validation, your toddler develops a strong sense of self-esteem and belief in their abilities. When you consistently express pride and admiration for your child's accomplishments, the toddler internalizes these messages and feels valued and capable.

Better Social Skills

A child who observes their parent resolving conflicts peacefully and showing empathy toward others is more likely to exhibit similar behaviors in their own social interactions.

Science-Based Information

Attachment Theory

Research in attachment theory highlights the importance of secure parent-toddler attachments in promoting healthy development. When parents respond consistently and sensitively to the toddler's needs, it creates a secure attachment and a foundation for emotional well-being and resilience throughout life. Toddlers with secure attachments are more likely to perform better in academics, develop better social competence, and keep their mental health in check.

Neuroscience

Studies in neuroscience demonstrate that praise and encouragement can impact brain development. When your toddler receives positive feedback, the brain releases chemicals like dopamine and oxytocin, which are associated with pleasure, bonding, and motivation. This reinforces positive behaviors and strengthens the parent-child bond.

Behavioral Psychology

Research in behavioral psychology supports the effectiveness of positive reinforcement in shaping desired behaviors. When parents consistently reward and reinforce positive actions, they increase the likelihood of those behaviors being repeated. This creates a cycle of positivity where your toddler feels motivated to continue making positive choices.

Longitudinal Studies

Longitudinal studies have also highlighted that toddlers who experience positive parenting practices perform better across various domains of development. These include higher academic achievement, fewer behavioral problems, healthier relationships, and greater overall well-being. Nevertheless, positive parenting sets your toddler on a trajectory for success and fulfillment in life.

Continuous Learning in Parenting

Parenting is a long journey that unfolds over a lifetime, marked by moments of joy, challenges, and endless opportunities for growth. On the basic level, it is a journey of self-awareness, reflection, and adaptation, where no parent is expected to be perfect. Instead, the key lies in recognizing that imperfection is a natural part of the parenting experience and that the true measure of success lies in your willingness to learn, grow, and evolve. Although every parent's challenges and experiences are unique, here are a few aspects you must keep in mind while navigating this complex and ever-evolving responsibility.

Embracing Imperfection

No parent is immune to the trials and tribulations of parenting. There will be days filled with laughter, triumphs, and moments of frustration and doubt. It's essential to acknowledge that making mistakes is inevitable. However, how you respond to these challenges truly matters. When you embrace imperfection as a fundamental aspect of the parenting journey, you can free yourself from unrealistic expectations and allow room for self-compassion and growth.

Learning from Experiences

Every interaction with your toddler offers valuable lessons and insights that can shape your parenting approach. Whether it's a moment of conflict, a milestone reached, or a simple gesture of love, each experience is an opportunity for reflection and learning. By approaching these experiences with an open mind and a willingness to grow, you can glean wisdom and deepen your understanding of yourself and your toddler.

Seeking Support When Needed

Parenting can be a challenging and isolating journey at times but remember that you don't have to navigate it alone. Seeking support from friends, family, and fellow parents can provide invaluable encouragement, perspective, and guidance. Whether it's joining a parenting group, seeking advice from a trusted mentor, or simply venting to a friend, reaching out for support is a sign of strength, not weakness.

Moving Forward with Positivity

When setbacks inevitably occur, approach them with a positive mindset and a commitment to growth. Instead of dwelling on past mistakes or perceived shortcomings, focus on what can be learned from the experience and how it can inform your parenting approach moving forward. Embracing each setback will become an opportunity for growth and improvement, knowing that resilience is born from adversity.

Striving for Positive Parenting

Above all, strive to cultivate a positive parenting approach grounded in love, empathy, and respect. Cherish the developmental milestones, practice gratitude for the moments of connection, and extend grace to yourself and your toddler when things don't go as planned. This will be the groundwork for a lifelong journey of learning, love, and mutual growth.

In parenting, imperfection is not a flaw to be erased but a thread that adds depth, resilience, and beauty to the journey. Embrace the messiness, celebrate the victories, and remember that the true measure of success lies not in perfection but in your willingness to show up, learn, and love with all your heart.

Chapter 3: Positive Discipline Methods

Discipline is often viewed as a combination of punishment and rewards. This approach works to adjust behavior at the moment, but the long-term consequences are not the greatest. A punitive approach to discipline does not consider the crucial life skills of reasoning, self-regulation, problem-solving, and communication. Positive discipline refocuses on instilling skills and values rather than preventing misbehavior.

Discipline is often viewed as a combination of punishment and rewards.[6]

Positive discipline is the shift from preventing your child from doing what is wrong to actively teaching them to do the right thing. Using methods like positive reinforcement, redirection, and time-in strengthens the parental bond to build the trust that eases socialization. Through the connection constructed by positive discipline techniques, you guide your child's character development.

Some maladaptive personality traits that carry over into adulthood were created by the prison warden framework of parenting that many have traditionally embraced. This short-sighted leadership through anxiety does not sow the seeds for healthy relationship development in the future. The early years of childhood have lasting impacts.

Centering your child's discipline on empathy, understanding, and guidance promotes self-discipline, responsibility, and respect. Using discipline to nurture these qualities forms a platform for your child to develop an independent social compass. So, instead of bending your child with firm wire, you throw compost in the garden for them to grow.

Punishment-Based Methods Versus Positive Parenting

The fundamental difference between punishment and guidance is that one exerts tyrannical control while the latter teaches self-control. Punishment is not rooted in discipline. A parent's frustration and anger are channeled into making a child pay for their mistake. This moral expectation is a distorted measurement because the parental role is more similar to a coach than a police officer.

On a basketball team, every player has unique skills and qualities. A good coach notices each player's potential and aims to elevate it. Additionally, the coach will examine what motivates each player and their temperaments. In this way, he can take the correct approach to each player to guide them toward winning and also allow them to learn in their own way.

If you apply this sports analogy to positive discipline, you coach your child about the socially acceptable ways to express themselves. They learn the appropriate way to engage with the world and look to you as their predominant guide. Their mind is wired to learn what they should do. Focusing on what they cannot do creates confusion. As their parental coach, you are explaining the rules of this new game of life. If these rules are introduced to your children harshly, they will be resistant to playing the game.

The scale of punishment and reward has been the predominant parenting go-to for decades. Breaking free from this deeply entrenched framework can be difficult. It feels intuitive to embrace punishment as a corrective measure. However, children who are constantly punished think that there is something inherently wrong with them instead of understanding that they are making detrimental decisions.

Positive discipline teaches children how to think instead of what to think. The internal emotional space and the external world of constant stimuli can be overwhelming for a toddler. Their reactions are driven by impulse and ignorance instead of malicious intent. A correction in direction can be more helpful than a punishment, considering that a child is not acting this way to hurt or annoy you.

Instead of controlling your child, you can manipulate their environment for them to have a safe space to explore their thoughts and feelings. An unfulfilled need drives negative behavior. Children do not yet have the words to explain what's bothering them – half the time, adults can't do it either.

Positive discipline asserts that misbehavior is caused by misunderstanding. There may be a communication barrier, or your child may not grasp what kind of behavior is expected in a social context. For example, your toddler may be crawling under the table at dinner time. When people are settling down to eat at night, it is not the appropriate time for hide-and-seek. Instead of yelling at the child about what they are not supposed to do, a caregiver can invite the child to participate. They can ask, "Do you want to help me take out your plate for dinner?"

Positive discipline works by dissecting the psychological processes of learning and framing behavior correction through this informed lens. Toddler behaviors like temper tantrums, hitting, and disobedience can be diminished when you become the emotional and behavioral training wheels they need.

Punishments bypass the reasoning process. A toddler has no self-determination in the punishment process. They avoid negative behavior because of fear instead of desiring to do the right thing. When toddlers gain fulfillment from a behavior, they are more likely to pursue it.

Your discipline techniques should create the conditions to learn. Your actions may inadvertently bypass the verbal lessons you want to teach. Your interactions and behaviors are like subconscious lectures. Positive parenting is a participatory model. These techniques only work with repetition, mindfulness, and constant reinforcement.

This approach is relationship-based. The empathetic and communicative connection facilitated by using these techniques will smoothly guide you through all the developmental milestones. As much as your mind is buzzing with the anxieties of raising a young child, your toddler faces the anxiety of absorbing a flurry of new information.

Punishment comes from the egoic assertion that a parent stands in the position of an all-knowing and all-powerful authority. The individual experience of a child is not taken into account as they are shoved by fear and violence into an uncomfortable mold. Mindfully disciplining a child acknowledges their needs and desires so that you can craft your boundaries around creating an optimal environment for all.

This approach to discipline eradicates the notion of a child not doing something because their parents will get angry. The positive reframing of discipline as guidance replaces punishment with education. Resultantly, you extend your child's horizons by compassionately introducing them to social protocols.

Long-Term Methods of Toddler Discipline

Positive discipline requires consistently applying five main practices. These categories aim to facilitate a healthy parental bond by creating mutual understanding, building independence, and making expectations clear. Punishment as discipline is lopsided. It professes to instill positive behavior by using verbal and sometimes physical violence. Using undesirable behavior like yelling to produce desirable outcomes seems self-defeating.

To prevent this mixed messaging to toddlers, you must consider communication, boundaries, modeling, expectations, and transforming mistakes into lessons. Grasping each of these aspects of positive discipline allows parents to create an environment for liberating education instead of anxiety-inducing constrictive eggshells to walk around.

Communication

Communication is the cornerstone of positive discipline. With all the varying perceptions, upbringings, and experiences, communication among adults is complicated. These complications are exponentially multiplied when dealing with a toddler. With grown-ups, there are overlapping spheres of expectations during interpersonal exchanges. With a toddler, these spheres do not yet exist. Therefore, the communication you participate in becomes highly specialized.

Communication is the cornerstone of positive discipline.[7]

Toddlers may communicate physically or emotionally because their vocabulary is still limited. They scream their point across or cry their discomfort. You create mutual understanding by becoming a filter for these raw expressions. You give your toddler the labels, words, and appropriate ways to express their needs, thoughts, and feelings by walking through their experiences with them.

Boundaries

A toddler cannot yet understand concepts like rules or boundaries. They are wired to push against the barriers and see how far the world can expand. Simply explaining rules to a toddler will not work in these early years. Therefore, boundaries are positively reinforced by redirecting away from an unwanted behavior to something more desirable. You can create boundaries according to your toddler's needs. For example, toddlers are naturally curious and love to explore. Therefore, you can create curated spaces where they can exercise more freedom, like a playroom.

Boundaries are created with rules. For a toddler to grasp how rules create cohesion, patience, and repetition are required. You may want to create an environment where everyone speaks respectfully. So, you will need to constantly remind your toddler to speak calmly and use polite words like "please" and "thank you." Take your child's attention span into account. It is best to create simple boundaries with one-step instructions like "You can only play on the porch."

Modeling

Your child is constantly watching. They receive the bulk of their social cues from you. Considering that your child is persistently stalking you like a prey animal, positive discipline requires self-control. You embody what you want to see in them. For example, if you want your child to be polite, say please and thank you when you talk to them.

Pretending is a brilliant way to model the behavior your child should exhibit. Playing with dolls, setting up scenarios, and showing your child what is expected through play solidifies the lesson, allowing them to internalize it. This combination of education, bonding, and play ensures that modeling has a lasting impact.

Expectations

Instead of the prohibitions that punishments create, positive reinforcement can build expectations so that your child begins developing a role in the family. Feeling included is a core need of all people; no one wants to be undervalued. You integrate your child into a positive identity with expectations.

Expectations are sown into daily routines. By creating predictability with a routine, a child begins to understand what is expected of them. In new environments, creating expectations can be difficult. In these unfamiliar contexts, you become your child's compass to help them understand the new rules of space. This is where spending time with your child is essential so that you can pick up on their emotional communication and actively shape their behavior according to your expectations.

Mistakes as Lessons

A mistake is not a trainwreck. Toddlers will make many mistakes. They stumble around a world they were dropped into a couple of years ago, so of course, they will bump into some things. Mistakes should be seen as learning opportunities. For example, if your toddler aggressively yanks a toy out of your hand and it breaks, you can teach them that they need to be gentle.

Walk them through the experience, addressing any negative emotions. Use prompts like "Your toy is broken now. Does that make you upset?" If they cry, console and affirm them. Let them know it is okay to have negative emotions. Then, explain to them why they need to be gentle with their toy to ingrain the lesson.

Empathy

This is one of the most important aspects of positive parenting. Getting on your child's level to comprehend their needs and desires opens a new world of perception for a parent. Your child does not see the world as you do and likely never will. They are an individual – one who is formulating their own opinions and perspectives. Making an effort to perceive from their view helps you understand their behavior better and what changes you can make to address any issues.

Sometimes, you hear parents say things like, "He cries for everything." This shows a lack of understanding about communication. The question must be asked: have you taught the child alternative ways to engage with the world? The only way you can speak your child's language to teach them regulation skills is through empathetic interaction.

The Skills Created with Positive Discipline

The purpose of positive discipline is to help your toddler develop life skills that will be useful in their adulthood. Many of the unfortunate habits and automated reactions that people have were created in childhood. They may not realize it, but responses to adverse situations are conditioned early on.

However, positive social skills are also developed from a young age.

The positive discipline model takes into account how personality traits and social skills develop. The method is geared toward enhancing essential life skills. Your toddler is around you 90% of the time. You are not nurturing them to be fully reliant on you. As they grow, there will be more distance from you as their parent. Instilling self-regulation, problem-solving, and communication skills helps them become socially adept and able to interact independently.

Self-regulation

For a toddler between one and three, self-regulation is not highly developed. You are starting with a blank slate. You are not only teaching your toddler how to regulate themself, but you are introducing them to the concept of self-regulation. How you respond to their discomfort will determine how they regulate themselves. The empathy promoted by the positive discipline approach develops the emotional intelligence needed to effectively manage their emotions and impulses.

The period from about four to 14 months is crucial. When parents are more responsive to the needs of toddlers, they learn to self-regulate better because they become in tune with how their desires and discomforts manifest. At the age of three, their observation becomes keener, so you provide the keys to self-regulation with your behavior. The consistent warmth that you express to your child will guide how well their regulation skills develop.

Audrey was almost two when her mother began weaning her off breast milk. This process came with a lot of distress. To help Audrey regulate these uncomfortable emotions, her mother created an imaginary model named Jenny. She was Audrey's big sister. Audrey's mother helped her through the negative emotions by bringing her attention to Jenny, the imaginary big sister who had already stopped drinking breast milk. This imaginary role model acted as a pull away from breast milk. Audrey learned to manage her emotions by keeping her focus on the goal of growing up like her imaginary big sister. Self-regulation was instituted as part of this traumatic transition to make the emotional ride smoother.

Problem-Solving

When you bark at a child to stop what they're doing immediately, they have no choice. Sometimes, it is required to immediately intervene, like when a child is reaching for a candle, but many times, the stakes are not that high. Presenting your child with a multitude of choices develops masterful problem-solving. Positive discipline teaches a child how to reason out the better pathway between numerous options.

Introducing your child to multiple ways of interfacing with their environment and emotions creates self-awareness. Decisions can be introduced into a child's life in many small ways. You can lay out three t-shirts and allow your child to pick which one they want to wear. You can introduce problems into their playtime by pretending. For example, you can make-believe that a doll wants to paint. Ask your child what the doll needs to complete this activity by providing multiple options like a shoe, a cup, and a paintbrush. If your child chooses the wrong object, guide them through the error by bringing their attention to it. Say something like, "Don't you think a paintbrush is better for painting than a cup?" You can demonstrate how it works for extra emphasis.

Communication

Positive discipline promotes constant communication, which bolsters your child's communication skills as a by-product. The effort to step into their world pays off because it models open and honest communication. Furthermore, the communication you facilitate allows your child to navigate themselves and understand how to compartmentalize their desires.

Interpersonal relationships cannot be strengthened without solid communication. Your child's ability to make friends and socialize is cultivated through positive parenting. They learn about various channels of communication and discover socially acceptable ways to make their feelings known and to assert their boundaries.

Practical Strategies for Positive Discipline

Talking about it and doing it are not the same. Positive discipline is void without practical ways to apply the framework. You can read a million articles on the theory, motivations, and benefits, but they are all fruitless if they cannot simply break down what you need to do. Positive discipline is complex because it is founded on relationships as well as how you and your child interact. These practices are like a beginner springboard that shows you how to get started in this dynamic process.

The following strategies are practical outlines of how you can apply positive discipline. You may fully understand the theory but framing it into actionable techniques may still escape you. These simple examples will guide you to take the first steps into your positive discipline journey. Institute these methods with patience and consistency and notice how they start manifesting over a few weeks.

Positive Reinforcement

Positive reinforcement is congratulating and rewarding behavior that you want to be repeated. With reinforcement, you indicate to your child how they should behave. This opens the doorway to the formation of positive habits.

Here are some tips to remember when using positive reinforcement:

- **Praise the Behavior Immediately.** When you notice that your child is doing something good, let them know when they are in the middle of the task or soon after they have completed it. This helps to establish the connection right away and brings their attention to what they are doing.
- **Use Various Kinds of Praise.** Communication happens on multiple levels. Praise your child with speech and touch. Encouraging words coupled with a high five or a hug do wonders to deeply ingrain the message.
- **Spend Time with Your Child.** When you spend quality time together, your child picks up on the behaviors that make you happy. Children are unexpectedly observant, so just by being around you and having your undivided attention, you can reinforce positive attitudes.

Redirection

A child's mind is constantly getting pulled in a million directions at once. They radically skip between thoughts and emotions, experiencing erratic ups and downs in a short time. Often, to prevent your child from behaving negatively, all it takes is a distraction. Redirecting your child is the process of showing them that they have better options.

- **Act Quickly.** Redirection works when you pull your child away from a trigger quickly. For example, if you see your child approaching the pot plant soil to make a horrific mess, redirect their attention to the playdough in your hand.
- **Understand your Child's Motivations.** Knowing what your child would prefer to do takes spending time with them. You may pick up that your child enjoys playing with wheels. When they are about to start acting out in a mall, you can pull a toy car from your pocket to divert their attention.

- **Be Aware of Your Child's Needs and Desires.** Your child may want to play actively, so they climb on the tables in the house. If you recognize that they want to climb, you can intervene by taking them outside or setting up more appropriate spaces for climbing in the home.

Time-in

Time-in is noticing when your child is beginning a cycle of distress so you can intervene before it gets out of hand. This technique works when you understand your child's triggers and patterns. This is why positive parenting requires you to be present and focused.

Time-in is noticing when your child is beginning a cycle of distress so you can intervene before it gets out of hand.'

- **Ask About Their Feelings.** Verbal communication can show a toddler you are concerned with them, allowing them to be more open.

- **Give Them Your Undivided Attention.** If you are multitasking or looking at your phone, your toddler will notice that your focus is not on them. This may cause them to take drastic action to get your attention. When you see an episode of distress brewing, it is best to focus wholly on your child.

- **Observe Their Body Language and Patterns.** Typically, there are signs that your child's behavior or mood will begin to shift. Preemptively acting when the cycle is in its early stages can prevent disaster.

Natural Consequences

Natural consequences are about allowing your child to experience the direct result of their actions at the moment. For example, your child may be crying to taste some apple cider vinegar even after you've told them that they won't like it. You then give them a spoon, and they hate the taste. Through that experience, they understand the limitations you set.

- **Create a Safe Environment.** To fully exploit nature's teaching mechanism, you need to be in a safe space where you can curate the environment and observe your child.

- **Do Not Belittle Your Child** After the Experience. Focus on the action rather than on how foolish they were for taking it. If you take the apple cider vinegar example again, instead of saying how silly they were for demanding a taste, ask them about the sensation so they can make the connections. Use questions like "How did it taste? Did you enjoy it? Can you see why I didn't want to give it to you?"

- **Give Your Child the Freedom to Explore.** The trope of the helicopter parent hovering around exists for a reason. You cannot stop your child from making every mistake. They need to develop their reasoning and processing abilities. If you step in at the smallest inconvenience, they become reliant on you instead of unfolding their experiences.

Modeling

You are your child's greatest hero. They care more about what you think and do than anybody else. Therefore, you are their primary example. Modeling allows you to reflect on behaviors you want to see in your toddler.

- **Play Imaginative Games.** Children engage with reality predominantly through play. If you can introduce lessons into their playtime, those lessons are significantly more likely to stick.

- **Be Mindful of Your Behavior, Tone, and Actions.** As a parent, you will get frustrated. Taking a few breaths before you respond so you can craft a well-thought-out reaction is transformational.

- **Ask Your Child to Join in When You are Busy with Activities.** If you see the opportunity to instill value in your child, extend the invitation for them to join. For example, if you are feeding your pet, ask your child if they would like to help. This will promote care for others and give them a sense of responsibility.

Parent-Child Cooperation

Implementing positive discipline reduces conflict through mutual understanding, and one of the primary pillars of positive discipline is communication. In the following chapter, you submerse yourself in the science of communication to master this core element of parenting. Through practical communication tips and in-depth exploration, you will be equipped to better understand your toddler and interpret their behavior.

Chapter 4: The Power of Positive Communication

You can't achieve positive and effective parenting without fostering positive communication lines with your child. After reading this chapter, you'll understand how positive communication can be the key to developing a stronger bond with your child and encouraging them to share their thoughts, feelings, and experiences with you. Approaching your child with empathy, tolerance, and understanding, which are aspects of positive communication, is crucial for your toddler's emotional development. This chapter explores what positive communication is and how it impacts your child's self-esteem. It also offers strategies and examples on how to practice positive communication and how doing so can benefit your toddler throughout different phases of their lives, from childhood to adulthood.

The key to effective parenting is understanding how to communicate with your child.[9]

What Is Positive Communication?

The key to effective parenting is understanding how to communicate with your child. You can't tell them what they should and shouldn't know or raise them to be successful and good individuals if you can't get through to them or don't give them the chance to communicate their thoughts and feelings. Therefore, fostering positive two-way channels of communication is crucial for nurturing children. The essence of positive parenting is to discipline your child and ensure they're well-behaved while enhancing their self-esteem and happiness.

Children's understanding of language is more advanced than their ability to use it effectively. Therefore, you need to be mindful of what you communicate to them and keep up with their linguistic development. The way you communicate can either hinder or improve your child's self-esteem, which is why you need to encourage, praise, and reassure your child consistently. When they misbehave, gently correct or ground them, depending on the severity of the situation, but without disrespecting them. This means you should avoid saying or doing things that make them question their worth. Your aim should always be helping your child grow and learn from their mistakes without negatively affecting their self-esteem.

Children shouldn't feel like your love is conditional. No one should feel the need to earn their parents' love, affection, and care. Otherwise, they'll grow up feeling inadequate and insecure. How your child behaves in the relationships they build during their adolescence and adulthood reflects the thoughts, feelings, and behaviors of their childhood. A person's self-concept, which is associated with how they perceive themselves and their roles in society, also develops between two and six years of age. This means that an adult's confidence, stress management, and self-motivation skills all stem from the environment in which they grew up.

How you raise your child and the relationship you build with them largely contributes to their self-concept. Criticizing, blaming, accusing, judging, and tearing your child down frequently is likely to cause them to question their worth, role, and importance in their community as adults.

How to Practice Positive Communication

Don't Tune Them Out and Give Them the Time of Day

Model the behaviors you wish to see your child do. If you want them to listen to you, you should also be a good listener to them. Many parents don't notice that they inadvertently tune out their children's chattering, especially if they're talkative. While this is understandable sometimes, particularly when you're busy, this shouldn't be a habit. Even if you throw in a "really?" or "hmm" here and there, children notice when others aren't focusing or seem to be disinterested. Over time, they'll feel like their experiences, thoughts, feelings, and concerns aren't important. Not only does this harm their self-esteem, but it also stops them from sharing things with you in the future. Your child might no longer come to you whenever they need help or are in trouble.

To positively communicate with your child, make a conscious effort to pay attention and actively listen to them whenever possible. If you're busy, they'll likely appreciate it if you tell them, "Hey, would you mind if we talk in a few minutes/hours when I'm done with this task? Or, is there something really important that you want to talk to me about right now?" instead of simply tuning them out. You can dedicate a specific time of day, such as an hour before their bedtime, to sit with your child and listen to everything they have to say. You should avoid doing anything else during the time you dedicate to your child.

Show Interest in What They Have to Say

Show interest in their ideas, thoughts, feelings, opinions, and experiences, and encourage them to share them with you. You can also take turns talking about your day with them to show them that communication is a two-way street, where both people should listen to each other.

When you're spending quality time with them, avoid correcting linguistic, vocabulary, or grammatical mistakes. Focus on what they're trying to say instead. Create a safe space where they feel comfortable to speak about their feelings without fear of overreaction or being judged. Give them enough time to communicate what they're trying to say without using body language that might be perceived as impatient, such as tapping your foot or sighing. Answer their questions to the best of your ability by using simple vocabulary. Keep in mind that if your child constantly interrupts conversations, this might be a sign that they're yearning for attention.

Show Them Appreciation

Praise them and tell them that you're proud of them whenever they engage in desirable behaviors. Mention that their actions make a difference and help others. For instance, if they tidy up their room, you can say, "Thank you so much for tidying up! I appreciate it. You know, I was just thinking about all the things I have to do. You just helped me cross a task off my list!" If they complement someone, you could say, "It's very kind of you to notice and praise good things in others. I bet you just made their day a lot better!" Praising good behavior and bringing attention to its value reinforces and encourages them to keep up their efforts.

Demonstrate Your Faith in Them

Show that you trust them and their abilities. You need to find the right balance between looking out for your child and making sure they have enough space to grow, learn, and experiment. If you constantly tell your child to be careful or that they'll hurt themselves, they will soon lose trust and confidence in themselves. Instead of constantly warning them, ask them about the risks associated with what they wish to do and how to reduce them.

For example, instead of telling your child to use a plastic knife, to which they might resist and throw a fit because they believe they can handle a metal knife, you can say, "I want to ask you a question before you use the knife. What bad thing might happen if you use the metal knife? It's very sharp; do you think it could slip and cut you?" When they respond, ask them how they think they can mitigate these risks, and they will likely suggest using a plastic knife. The key here is to guide them toward suggesting the alternatives themselves. In case of situations that won't cause severe harm, you can allow them to explore and take a degree of risks while supervising them and taking other measures to ensure their safety.

Offer the guidance they need while giving them enough space to do things by themselves. Make sure they also have all the knowledge and skills they need to do a certain task safely beforehand. Most importantly, lead by example. Demonstrate sound decision-making and mindful behaviors and actions to show them that adults are cautious and care about their safety as well. For example, if you switch off the stove, you can say, "I'd better let this pot cool off for a while before I pick it up so I don't get burned." Proceed to leave it for a few minutes before taking your oven mitts off to move the pot.

Allow Them to Do Things That Fuel Their Confidence

Give them the time of day to do things they're talented in and can do well. Remind them that they're competent in several areas of their lives. If they enjoy reading and are good at it, make sure they read a couple of pages before bed and praise their reading abilities. If they're talented in art, allow them to do a craft every day and express how much you like it.

Celebrate Efforts Rather Than Results

Praise and show pride in the effort they make, even if they don't yield the desired results. Teach your child that they should always give things their best effort, even if it doesn't guarantee success. They need to know that it's okay to fail as long as they give things an honest try. You should also avoid constantly criticizing and correcting their mistakes. Let things slide whenever you can.

Praise and show pride in the effort they make.[10]

Everyone, not just children, makes mistakes and goes through phases of trial and error. Toddlers continuously experiment because they don't know which actions will yield positive reactions and results and which ones won't. If you make remarks about everything, they might feel discouraged and avoid experimenting, which hinders self-growth and development.

Separate Your Child from Their Actions

Learn to separate your child from their actions. It can be difficult to avoid criticizing someone whenever they engage in behaviors that irritate you or ones that you disapprove of. However, learning to disapprove of the *activity* and not the *person* is crucial when you're dealing with a child. They have to know that your love for them is unconditional and that their wrongdoings don't take away any of their worth. For example, if your child insults someone, you can say, "Insulting someone was a very bad thing to do. You wouldn't like someone to say this to you, right? Good people treat others how they would like to be treated" instead of "You're a very impolite/bad child!"

Remind Them That You Love Them

Don't assume that your child knows how much you love, appreciate, and value them and how proud you are of them. Everyone needs reassurance from time to time. Telling them you love them and reminding them of how you feel about them often can boost their self-esteem and allow them to realize that they don't need to earn your love.

Use Positive Language

Use positive rather than negative language. Instead of telling your child what they shouldn't do, tell them what they should do. For example, saying, "Walk on the sidewalk beside me," is better than "Don't walk too near to the road." Positive language usually gives more precise instructions, is easy to remember, and helps eliminate confusion.

Be Mindful of Your Body Language

Children are smarter than what most people credit them for. You might be surprised as to how early they can pick up on nonverbal communication cues, such as body language and tone of voice. If you're being sarcastic or disinterested, for example, they would be able to tell that something is off even if they can't quite put their fingers on it. This is why, when talking to your child, you should be very mindful of your body language and other communication cues. Maintain eye contact with your toddlers so they know that you're paying attention to them. This is why you should always try to talk to them whenever you're not busy with something else. You should also avoid talking to them if you're facing the other way.

Smile and maintain an approachable facial expression when you're talking to them. Otherwise, they might wonder if you're upset with them, even if this isn't the case. You should also maintain a gentle tone of voice and your composure even if you're irritated. Losing your temper will keep them from sharing things with you in the future. Squat or sit down so that you're at the same level as your toddler when you're having a conversation. Children might feel intimidated or powerless when adults tower over them and will struggle to communicate their thoughts and feelings effectively. Hug your child and cuddle them often. Pat or console them when needed.

Seek Professional Help if Needed

Don't hesitate to reach out to a professional if you think that there are alarming communication difficulties on either end. If your child isn't speaking at all by the age of two, then they are conveying serious behavioral issues or engaging in recurrent defiant behaviors. If you notice speech difficulties like stuttering, suspect they have hearing difficulties or have other serious communication issues, you'll likely benefit from consulting a speech-language pathologist or a child psychologist, depending on the problem.

Seek professional help for extra guidance if you're feeling stuck.[11]

Additional Tips

- Avoid using forceful language, such as "You have to / should / must do this." Frame your commands as suggestions and brainstorm why doing these things would benefit them or their situation.

- If you must say "no" to something they're asking for, coming up with feasible alternatives or ways to compromise can avoid tantrums.

- Work together on finding the silver lining in any inconvenient situation.

- Focus on one point at a time when requesting or discussing things with your toddler. Make sure your conversations are specific and simple.

- If you plan on discussing difficult topics with your toddler, make sure to give them a heads-up beforehand. Letting them know what to expect allows them to feel prepared and more in control of the situation.

The Benefits of Communicating Positively with Your Toddler

They'll Learn to Communicate Positively with Others

Implementing positive communication strategies with your child can significantly improve their social skills. The way you communicate with your toddler serves as a blueprint as to how they should communicate with those around them. Positive communication ensures that you feel understood, that you understand others, respect other people's boundaries, express your thoughts, feelings, and ideas, engage in conversations, and partake in debates or negotiations without potentially disrespecting or attacking others.

When you communicate positively with your child, you teach them to discuss their concerns and dislikes without criticizing other people. This means of communication sets the stage for building and maintaining healthy interpersonal relationships in the long run. Positive communication will teach your child to navigate different types of social situations effectively, even when negative emotions such as discomfort or frustration arise. Learning how to communicate positively and effectively will allow your child to grow up feeling self-assured and confident. They'll be able to speak their mind without fearing hurting others or facing rejection.

It Reduces Resistance and Tantrums

Forcing your child to do certain things, bossing them around, criticizing them frequently, or always saying "no" without offering some sort of explanation only leads to stubbornness and resistance. Since adults naturally have authority over children, children usually feel lonely and powerless, which is why they throw temper tantrums or engage in rebellious behaviors.

A lack of mutual understanding and effective communication can create a gap between you and your child and negatively impact their self-esteem. By actively listening to your child, responding to their concerns soundly, and approaching them with empathy and tolerance, they will be more open to accepting your guidance and advice.

It Enhances Problem-Solving and Decision-Making Skills

Positive communication fosters problem-solving and decision-making skills. It's also a great way to make your toddler feel like they have some say over their actions and are being treated more like adults. The more you encourage your child to speak their mind and stop coddling them, the better they can develop and improve their language.

It will Lead to Academic Success

Children who can express themselves, share their ideas, and communicate effectively from a younger age are more likely to perform well in their academics. Children with good communication skills are better at grasping and retaining concepts and are more likely to partake in group projects and in-class discussions. They're also able to build and maintain better relationships with their peers and teachers, making their learning environment more conducive and supportive.

They will Become Self-Sufficient

Children with better communication skills are usually more independent. They are more effective at navigating difficult social situations, standing up for themselves, backing their opinions, building relationships with others, and ensuring that their boundaries aren't overstepped. When raised in an environment that encourages positive communication, children learn that needing guidance, advice, or clarification isn't a sign of weakness, and therefore, they are less likely to resist it or respond with anger.

They'll Enforce Strong and Healthy Boundaries

Teaching your child positive communication skills enhances their ability to look out for their mental and physical health. They easily realize when someone is overstepping their boundaries or negatively impacting their well-being. Their communication skills allow them to communicate their needs, expectations, and feelings in different types of relationships throughout their lives, ensuring that they feel valued, appreciated, understood, and comfortable when dealing with people they surround themselves with.

It Sets Them Up for Future Success

Effective communication skills set your child up for success in the future. When they know how to communicate with others, they'll succeed in their pursuit of higher education and various work environments. Communicating positively with your child also encourages them to treat themselves with kindness and compassion, which is needed throughout the different phases of their life. It also sets the standard for how others should treat them, which prevents them from settling in environments or with people who don't value or treat them as they should.

They Become Better at Solving Problems

Strong communication skills allow children to handle and resolve conflicts in rational and sound ways. They're able to diffuse tension and reach common ground without invalidating people's thoughts, feelings, and opinions. Teaching your child the basics of positive communication and modeling this behavior allows them to think critically and come up with helpful solutions to issues.

It Fosters Empathy

Positive communication also encourages your child to empathize with others and put themselves in their shoes to understand their perspectives and gain insight into their feelings. Understanding the interests of others encourages them to reach mutually satisfactory solutions instead of solely looking out for their own benefits. They learn how to be active listeners, maintain respectful and attentive body language, and engage in effective storytelling.

Now that you've read this chapter, you understand positive communication and how it can help your child grow, develop, and maintain good self-esteem. Positive communication is one of the cornerstones of your child's ability to maintain mental, emotional, physical, and social health. Move on to the next chapter for tips on how to build strong emotional bonds with your toddler.

Chapter 5: Building Strong Emotional Bonds with Your Little One

Parenting is an incredible journey filled with moments of joy, laughter, and challenges. As a parent, you may find yourself asking: How deep is my love for my child/children? It's a question that truly resonates when you go through the ups and downs of parenting, from those tender first moments holding your newborn to guiding your toddlers through their early years of discovery.

The value of a strong bond is priceless and will do wonders for your parenting journey.[12]

When you hold your newborn for the first time, you experience a love that knows no bounds. It's a bond that goes beyond words, a connection forged in the heart. This is unconditional love – a love that accepts, forgives, and nurtures without hesitation.

However, unconditional love is more than just warm, fuzzy feelings. It's a commitment to selflessness, respecting your children for who they are, and providing them with the guidance and support they need to grow.

As your child grows, so too does your love. From nurturing infants to guiding toddlers through the beginnings of discipline and play, each stage brings new challenges and opportunities for deeper connection.

This chapter will cover exactly why it's so important to form strong bonds with your toddlers and how essential it is for their development and well-being. You should never underestimate the power of unconditional love and how it can shape a positive parent-child relationship.

Early Emotional Development

From the moment they enter the world, infants are constantly learning and responding to the world around them. Have you ever noticed how some parents seem to be so in sync with their child's needs, almost as if they have a sixth sense? This attunement is a result of having a deep emotional connection with their child. However, if you feel like you don't have this level of connection with your child, there's still hope. You will need to first understand why it's such a big deal to form an emotional connection with your toddler, who barely understands how anything in the world works.

Emotional development in the early years lays the foundation for a child's overall well-being. It's a lot like building the groundwork for a sturdy house – if the foundation is strong, the structure will stand tall and resilient against life's storms. You'd be surprised to find out that children have a strong sense of what's going on around them and how the people around them behave with them. Especially as toddlers, children are rapidly developing emotionally, forming the building blocks of their future relationships and emotional regulation skills.

Consider a newborn baby who cries when they're hungry or uncomfortable. Through their cries, they're communicating their needs, and how you respond sets the tone for their emotional development. By soothing and comforting them when they cry, you teach them that their feelings are valid and that they can trust you to meet their needs. This simple act creates a sense of security and lays the groundwork for a secure attachment.

Attachment Theory

Attachment theory was proposed by psychologist John Bowlby, suggesting that children form emotional bonds with their caregivers early in life, significantly influencing their social, emotional, and cognitive development. These bonds serve as a secure base from which children can explore the world around them and seek comfort when needed.

Attachment theory becomes especially relevant to toddlers as they navigate the transition from infancy to early childhood. Toddlers are at a crucial developmental stage where they're beginning to assert their independence while still relying heavily on their caregivers for support and guidance.

At this age, toddlers are exploring their environment with newfound curiosity and enthusiasm. They may toddle off to explore a new toy or investigate a fascinating object, but they often look back to their caregiver for reassurance and validation. This behavior is known as "secure base behavior," where toddlers use their attachment figure as a safe haven from which to explore and return when they need comfort or support.

For example, imagine taking your toddler to a crowded playground for the first time. As they venture off to explore the swings and slides, they periodically glance back to make sure you're still nearby. They may rush back to you for assistance and reassurance if they encounter a challenge, like difficulty climbing a ladder or navigating a crowded area. This back-and-forth between exploration and seeking comfort illustrates the secure base provided by the caregiver, which allows the toddler to explore their surroundings confidently.

Attachment theory can also help you understand the different attachment styles that toddlers may show. The most desirable attachment style is secure attachment, characterized by a strong bond with the caregiver, trust in their availability and responsiveness, and the ability to explore independently while knowing the caregiver is there for support.

However, not all toddlers develop secure attachments. Some may adopt insecure attachment styles, like anxious-ambivalent attachment or avoidant attachment, which can arise from inconsistent caregiving, neglect, or other factors. These insecure attachment styles may manifest as clinginess, difficulty separating from the caregiver, or a lack of trust in the caregiver's availability and responsiveness.

Understanding attachment theory can help you support healthy attachment relationships with your toddler. By providing consistent love, support, and responsiveness, you can create a secure attachment that lays the foundation for positive social and emotional development.

Think about a toddler who toddles over to you with outstretched arms, seeking comfort after a small tumble. Their instinctual need for reassurance and safety is a testament to the attachment bond they've formed with you. When you respond with warmth and empathy, you will reinforce their sense of security and teach them that they can rely on you for support.

Building Secure Attachments

The bond between a parent and their child shapes the child's emotional and psychological development, as well as their sense of security, trust, and self-worth. Building secure attachments with your toddler lays the groundwork for a lifetime of healthy relationships and emotional resilience.

Parental Presence and Responsiveness

Parental presence and responsiveness are the cornerstones of building secure attachments with toddlers. Imagine a toddler who calls out for their caregiver after stumbling and scraping their knee. The caregiver's immediate response, whether it's offering comforting words, a gentle touch, or a comforting hug, communicates to the child that their needs are important and that they can rely on their caregiver for support.

Presence goes beyond physical proximity – it's about being emotionally attuned to the child's needs and providing a sense of security and stability in their environment. This might involve being fully present during playtime, mealtime, or bedtime routines, engaging in meaningful interactions, and actively listening to the child's cues and expressions.

Responsiveness is equally crucial, as it demonstrates to the child that their caregiver is attuned to their needs and will provide comfort and support when needed. Whether it's responding promptly to cries of distress, offering words of encouragement during challenging moments, or simply being available to listen and connect, responsiveness fosters a sense of trust and security in the parent-child relationship.

Security in Parent-Child Relationships

Trust and security are the building blocks of a healthy parent-child relationship, laying the foundation for secure attachments to form. When children feel safe and secure in their relationship with their caregiver, they're more likely to explore the world with confidence, knowing that their caregiver is there to support and protect them.

Think about a toddler who hesitantly approaches a new playmate at the park. Their caregiver's reassuring presence gives them the confidence to interact with others and explore new social situations. This sense of security empowers the child to take risks, learn from their experiences, and develop crucial social and emotional skills.

Trust is earned through consistent caregiving, reliability, and unconditional love. When caregivers consistently meet the child's needs, respond to their cues, and provide a nurturing and supportive environment, the child learns to trust in the caregiver's availability and responsiveness. This trust forms the bedrock of secure attachments, fostering a deep and enduring bond between parent and child.

Healthy Emotional Bonds

Attachment theory provides valuable insights into the dynamics of parent-child relationships and the formation of secure attachments. At its core, attachment theory emphasizes the importance of a child's early experiences with their caregiver in shaping their social, emotional, and cognitive development.

Secure attachment, characterized by trust, security, and emotional closeness, lays the groundwork for healthy emotional bonds and positive relationship outcomes later in life. When caregivers provide consistent love, support, and responsiveness, children develop a secure base from which to explore the world and form meaningful connections with others.

Conversely, insecure attachment styles, such as anxious-ambivalent or avoidant attachment, can arise from inconsistent caregiving, neglect, or other factors. These insecure attachment patterns may lead to difficulties in regulating emotions, forming healthy relationships, and navigating social situations effectively.

Practical Strategies for Daily Connection

How can you deepen your bond and show unconditional love to your child? You might already give your child hugs and meet their basic needs, but how do you take it to the next level? Your child grows so fast – from a tiny baby to an active toddler – in just a couple of years. The sooner you build that strong connection, the sooner you can enjoy positive parenting moments.

As your child grows and learns, there are countless ways to strengthen your bond through family activities and quality time together. These simple suggestions can make a big difference in your child's physical, emotional, and social development, especially during their early years of growth. And, the best part? You can do them right in the comfort of your own home. So, let's explore some easy ways to infuse your home environment with unconditional love and deepen your connection with your child.

Physical Connection

Nurturing your bond with your child involves more than just words – it's about physical gestures that convey love and support. Keep the physical connection alive by embracing your child with hugs, gentle pats on the back, or a reassuring ruffle of their hair. These small acts communicate a powerful message: "I'm here for you, always."

Constant physical affection is just as necessary as verbal assurance.[13]

Take time to share moments of closeness, such as snuggling together for an evening storytime session. The warmth of your embrace and the sound of your voice create a comforting cocoon of love and security for your child. Through these simple yet meaningful interactions, you reinforce the message that they are cherished and valued.

Additionally, don't underestimate the power of physical touch in everyday interactions. Whether it's a hug when saying goodbye in the morning or a high-five to celebrate a small victory, these moments of connection strengthen your bond with your child and foster a sense of belonging.

Moreover, remember the importance of eye contact and a warm smile in your interactions with your child. These nonverbal cues convey love, acceptance, and encouragement, reinforcing the emotional connection between you. Even a simple wave from across the room can brighten your child's day and remind them that they are loved and supported.

Prioritize Playtime

Playing with your child is not just to keep them busy and get them tired enough to fall asleep at night; it's also a powerful way to strengthen your bond and support their learning and development. When you actively participate in playtime with your child, you're not just a spectator; you're an active participant in their world, building a strong connection along the way.

Play is the language of childhood, and when you join in, you're speaking their language fluently. Whether you're building towers with blocks, putting together puzzles, or pretending to be superheroes, you're not just sharing a game; you're sharing moments of joy, laughter, and discovery.

Through play, children learn important skills like problem-solving, creativity, and social interaction. When you play alongside your child, you're not only supporting their learning but also deepening your bond with them. Sharing in their excitement and enthusiasm as they explore the world around them creates lasting memories and strengthens your connection.

Take time to celebrate the small victories together, whether it's completing a puzzle or successfully stacking blocks to build a tower. Share in their laughter and excitement, and don't forget to give plenty of high fives for a job well done. These simple gestures of encouragement reinforce the bond between you and let your child know that you're proud of their accomplishments.

Quality Time

When spending time with your child, make it truly quality time – time that is fully dedicated to them without distractions. It's easy to get caught up in the hustle and bustle of daily life, but carving out uninterrupted moments with your child is essential for building a strong and lasting connection.

Put away the distractions, especially your mobile phone. Your child deserves your full attention, not just a fraction of it while you're scrolling through notifications. By setting aside your phone and other distractions, you show your child that they are your priority and that you value your time together.

Even if your schedule is packed, remember that quality trumps quantity. It's better to have shorter periods of focused attention with your child than long stretches of distracted or half-hearted interaction. Whether it's 10 minutes of playing a game together or sharing a quick snack-time chat, make those moments count by being fully present and engaged.

Uninterrupted time with your child allows for deeper connections to form and meaningful conversations to take place. It's during these moments of undivided attention that you can truly connect with your child, understand their thoughts and feelings, and create lasting memories together.

Create an Emotional Connection

Acknowledging your child's feelings is not just about validating their emotions – it's about creating a deeper understanding and connection between the two of you. When you take the time to listen and empathize with your child's feelings, you create a safe space for them to express themselves authentically.

Emotional connection begins with empathy. By tuning into your own feelings and being in touch with your emotions, you set an example for your child to follow. When they see you express empathy and understanding toward others, they learn to do the same, fostering a sense of emotional intelligence and compassion.

When your child shares their feelings with you, whether it's excitement, sadness, or frustration, take the time to really listen. Show them that their emotions matter and that you're there to support them through every high and low. By acknowledging their feelings, you validate their experiences and strengthen the bond between you.

Empathy is the bridge that connects hearts and minds, allowing you and your child to truly understand each other on a deeper level. As you navigate the ups and downs of life together, this emotional connection becomes a source of strength and comfort, enriching your relationship and creating a bond that withstands the test of time.

Dinner Time

Dinner time isn't just about getting food inside your body. It is also a precious opportunity to nourish your relationships with your loved ones. Gathering around the table as a family provides the perfect setting for meaningful interactions and shared experiences.

Encourage family meals as a time to come together, sit around the table, and connect with one another. Whether it's a home-cooked meal or takeout pizza, the important thing is that you're all together, sharing in each other's company.

During dinner, take the time to talk about your day and encourage your children to do the same. Ask open-ended questions like, "What was the best part of your day?" or "Did anything funny happen at school?" These prompts invite conversation and help everyone feel included in the discussion.

Engage in active listening and show genuine interest in what each family member has to say. This isn't just about going through the motions; it's about truly connecting with one another and building stronger bonds as a family.

Use dinner time as an opportunity to teach valuable lessons about communication, respect, and family values. Model good behavior by taking turns speaking, listening attentively, and showing appreciation for one another.

Bedtime

Bedtime is a magical time to connect with your child and express your love in gentle, comforting ways. As the day winds down, the bedtime routine offers a precious opportunity to create lasting memories and strengthen your bond with your little one.

Embrace the bedtime routine as a special time to share stories, cuddles, and quiet moments together. Whether it's reading a favorite bedtime story or simply snuggling up for a few minutes of quiet reflection, these moments of closeness help your child feel safe, loved, and cherished.

Take advantage of this time by choosing books that spark joy and capture your child's imagination. It doesn't matter if you read the same story night after night; children find comfort in the familiarity and repetition of their favorite tales. The important thing is that you're sharing this time together, creating cherished memories that will last a lifetime.

Use bedtime as an opportunity to nurture your child's love of reading and storytelling. Encourage them to choose their favorite books and take turns reading aloud to each other. This not only fosters a love of literacy but also strengthens the bond between you as you share in the joy of storytelling.

In addition to reading, bedtime is a time for quiet reflection and intimate conversations. Take the opportunity to ask your child about their day, listen to their thoughts and feelings, and reassure them of your love and support. These moments of connection help your child feel understood, valued, and deeply connected to you.

Play Outside

Venturing outdoors and engaging in physical activity together is not only a fantastic way to connect with your child but also a wonderful opportunity to show them your love and support. Whether you're running, kicking a ball, or exploring nature together, these shared experiences strengthen your bond and create lasting memories.

Playing outdoors allows your toddler to connect with you and with nature, too.[14]

Embrace outdoor play as a chance to let loose, have fun, and enjoy each other's company. Head to the local park, where you can swing, slide, and climb together or explore nature trails and scenic spots in your area. The great outdoors provides a rich backdrop for adventure and discovery, sparking your child's imagination and fostering a sense of wonder.

Take the time to learn new activities together, whether it's flying a kite, playing catch, or riding bikes. These shared experiences not only promote physical health and well-being but also strengthen your emotional connection as you support and encourage each other along the way.

As you engage in outdoor play and exercise, keep the focus on enjoyment and togetherness rather than on competition. While a friendly game of tag or a soccer match can be exhilarating, be mindful not to impose too much pressure or expectation on the activity. The goal is to have fun, bond with your child, and create positive memories together.

Practicing unconditional love at home may feel more natural, but it's equally important to carry that sense of love and connection with you wherever you go. Whether you're out and about or your child is starting school, staying emotionally connected can pose challenges, but it's essential for nurturing a strong bond and supporting your child's growth and development.

When you're away from the familiar surroundings of home, it's important to prioritize open communication and empathy with your child. Listen to their thoughts and feelings, validate their experiences, and show understanding and support even in unfamiliar or challenging situations.

As you navigate the ups and downs of daily life, there may be times when you feel angry or frustrated. In these moments, it's crucial to remember your deep conviction about unconditional love and discipline. Discipline isn't about punishment; it's about teaching and guiding your child with love and empathy. By setting clear boundaries and expectations, you help your child learn valuable life lessons and develop essential skills for navigating the world around them.

Maintaining an aura of unconditional love requires consistency, patience, and understanding, even in the face of adversity. It's about showing your child that your love is unwavering, regardless of the circumstances, and that you're always there to support and guide them through life's challenges.

So, whether you're at home, out in public, or your child is starting school, let love be your guiding force. Embrace each moment as an opportunity to connect, teach, and nurture your child's growth and development. Through love, empathy, and discipline, you lay the foundation for a strong and enduring bond that will withstand the test of time.

Chapter 6: Boundaries that Empower

Imagine your child is walking toward an open fireplace. You tell them not to do so in a calm and kind voice. If they continue walking, you become stern and hold them back. When they ask why, you say that it's wrong. This is how many parents discipline their children.

Setting boundaries is important for keeping your toddler safe and also for having a healthy relationship with them as they grow.[15]

However, this strategy has a major flaw. While children know what wrong means, they may not understand why it's wrong or what to do next. By saying, "Don't do it," you are simply halting that action without giving a valid reason and not suggesting what they should do instead.

Try setting and explaining boundaries rather than vague disciplines and controlling behavior. It will teach your toddler to make responsible decisions, develop self-regulation, and learn to respect others from the heart.

Boundaries vs. Control

Setting boundaries seems like you're controlling your child's behavior, but they are two vastly different things. Controlling behavior is seen among authoritarian parents who set strict rules without giving any explanations. Boundaries are simply your way of saying you don't accept their behavior and explaining why you don't accept it. You are allowing your little ones to make their own decision without controlling their actions.

For example, when you say, "Don't do it, it's wrong," you're leaning more toward controlling behavior. When you say, "Don't do it because fire is hot and it will burn you," it makes you a more compassionate parent. Setting boundaries is more than just saying, "Don't do this/that;" providing reasoning adds a bit of compassion.

Why Establish Healthy Boundaries

Is your child doing something you don't want them to do, like refusing to share their toys during a playdate? There are two ways to go about this. You can either force them to share or set rules about sharing and explain the reasons. Both ways are effective, but the former may have a negative impact on their mental health.

By establishing healthy boundaries, on the other hand, you are not only caring for their mental health but also helping them grow into responsible adults. You are showing them that you care about them and also trust them to make the right decision.

- Boundaries help keep your toddler safe by preventing them from engaging in risky behaviors or activities that could harm them. For example, setting boundaries around dangerous objects like knives or electrical outlets protects them from accidents.

- You can use boundaries to teach your child about social norms and acceptable behavior. Say you're letting them borrow or share only one toy at a time. By taking turns sharing toys, they will communicate with their fellow children and learn to cooperate with them. Simple social skills taught at an early age will make them more outgoing and self-aware in the future.

- Your child may see the presence of boundaries as a secure cocoon that brings order to their chaotic life. This predictability will reduce their anxiety and frustration as they learn how to manage emotions at a very young age.

- Children may show only happiness or sadness by laughing or crying, but they experience a wide range of emotions. They just don't know how to regulate them, so they may keep crying or laughing for long hours without a reason. Boundaries help them regulate their emotions because they know exactly what to expect if they choose to do something.

- When you set boundaries, you teach your little one to become independent. They will learn to make certain decisions on their own and accept the consequences of choosing wrongly without showing resentment. For instance, if they think of refusing to share their toys with someone, they know that others won't let them borrow their toys. Though the negative thought may have crossed their mind, they will choose to share.

- Setting boundaries is one of the first steps toward developing healthy relationships. When you teach your child to respect boundaries, they will grow up setting and honoring boundaries in all their relationships, which will help them build a lasting bond with everyone around them.

Conflicts between toddlers and parents are common, but with the presence of rules and boundaries, you can teach your child how to resolve those conflicts on their own. For example, when they want another child's toy, they may throw a tantrum if you haven't set boundaries for sharing, like give and take. It's not their fault because they don't know how to get that toy. On the other hand, a child who has learned to respect healthy boundaries won't think twice before sharing their toys to get what they want.

Role of Consistent Boundaries

Consistent boundaries create a sense of security and predictability in your toddler's life. Hands-on experience also does that, but it can be dangerous. Imagine your child sees fire for the first time. Their curiosity will naturally prompt them to touch the flames. They will experience the heat when they come close, but they may not stop, not knowing what will happen.

When they touch the flames and feel the burning pain, they will realize that playing with fire is bad. Why make them go through that pain when you can set boundaries, explain the reasons, and prevent it from happening?

When boundaries are consistently enforced, your toddler learns what is expected of them in different situations. They understand what behaviors are acceptable and what behaviors are not. This clarity reduces confusion and anxiety, as they know what to anticipate in a given situation.

Boundaries are like a safety bubble for children. Knowing the limits and rules of their environment helps them feel secure and protected. This sense of safety allows them to explore and engage with their surroundings more confidently. Even if they are surrounded by danger, they will know exactly what to do to keep themselves safe. For example, if they are playing at the top of a hill, boundaries will help them know that going near the sides is dangerous, so they will keep to the middle of the hill to ensure their safety.

Predictability is another major benefit of having consistent boundaries. They establish a routine in your little one, such as meal times, bedtimes, and play times. Predictable routines provide a set structure to their day, which can comfort them even when you aren't around. Routines help them understand what comes next so they can avoid confusion and stress and bring stability to their lives.

Consistently enforcing boundaries also shows them they can trust you. It helps them believe in the fact that you're dependable. When you follow through with consequences for breaking the rules, they learn to trust that you will provide guidance and support when needed. This childhood trust will go a long way in securing your parent-child relationship in the future.

Practical Strategies and Tips for Setting Boundaries That Empower

Setting boundaries doesn't mean you write down a strict set of rules and narrate them to your little one. They may not understand half of what you said, and what they do understand, they may not accept it. Imagine your child is playing with their LEGO blocks by throwing them at the wall instead of building something. You show them the right way to build, but they don't listen and continue their throwing activity. This is when boundaries come into the picture.

If you simply state what is to be done, like "LEGOs are for building things, not throwing around," they may understand you but may not do as you said. Follow it up with an action or a consequence, like locking the game in your cupboard. The next day, they may repeat the same thing, but don't be disheartened. Keep the blocks out of their reach until they learn how to play with them; they will eventually learn.

Your basic strategy will be to tell your child what you want them to do, explain the reasons, and set rules and consequences for not doing it. Here are all the practical tips and strategies to implement your basic strategy and for setting empowering boundaries:

- **Establishing Rules:** This is the first step of setting boundaries for your child. They should understand the rules, so keep them clear and simple. Don't state multiple rules at the same time, like, "Brush your teeth, have a bath, and then you can eat." Toddlers cannot grasp more than one instruction at a time.

  Give them time to understand what to do one by one. Tell them to brush their teeth first and explain why they should. If they are hungry, let them know that their food will taste even more delicious after brushing their teeth. Let them understand and accept the rule and implement the suggestion before moving on to the next rule.

- **Using Positive Language:** Your child is in the toddler stage, an age of extensive learning. They are trying to understand new words and phrases as they associate them with different actions. They may know what negative words mean, like "don't," "no," or "quit," but they may not be able to associate them with other words.

  For instance, when you say, "Don't run," they may only register the word "run," and thus, keep running. Give a positive twist to your instructions and suggestions. Say "Please walk" instead of "Don't run," "Use your indoor voice" in place of "Stop yelling," and "Gentle touches only" instead of "No hitting."

- **Including Polite Affirmations:** If you want your child to become a polite and kind adult, include polite affirmations while setting boundaries for your toddler. It's often hard to maintain calmness while dealing with their tantrums. Practicing politeness greatly helps in regulating your emotions and theirs. It also teaches them to be polite in turn.

  Use basic polite affirmations like please, sorry, and thank you in your conversations with your little one. If they are hitting someone, say, "Please use gentle touches only." When they stop hitting, don't forget to say, "Thank you."

- **Explaining the Reasons:** The rules for boundaries, though easy to follow, can be hard to understand. "Please walk" is a straightforward instruction, but your child will wonder, why walk when they can *run?* Follow it up with an explanation like, "If you run, you will fall down and hurt yourself."

  Toddlers aren't mindless robots to keep doing as instructed. They are curious about the world around them and always eager to learn. Satiate their curiosity by giving explanations while setting boundaries. It will also help build trust and mutual respect.

- **Using Visual Aids:** For toddlers who can't yet read, use pictures or drawings to illustrate rules. You can create a visual chart with images representing acceptable and unacceptable behaviors. For example, you can show a child a picture of hitting and getting hit and mark a large red "X' on it. Then, show a child playing happily with other children with their arms on each other's shoulders. Embrace positivity by showing the image with unacceptable behavior only once and keeping the positive image regular.

- **Empathizing:** While it's important to be firm with boundaries, also show empathy and understanding toward your toddler's feelings. Say that you understand they are upset, but it doesn't mean they should hurt others. Emphasize the importance of using gentle touches while playing.

- **Offering Choices:** When you give your child a choice, you are showing you trust them to make their own decisions. They feel more valued and empowered. Also, you get a chance to keep the range of choices within the boundary you wish to set. For instance, if you don't want them to wear an overused green shirt, you can ask, "Would you like to wear the red shirt or the blue shirt today?"

- **Redirecting Attention:** Restricting an activity your toddler is doing may lead to unwanted tantrums. When you notice them engaging in an activity outside of the boundaries you set, gently redirect their attention to a more appropriate activity instead of saying, "Don't do that." Offer them a toy or suggest a different activity to focus on. You can also let them face the consequences of venturing outside the boundary, but it's better to try and redirect their attention first.

- **Using Positive Reinforcement:** This is an effective strategy for both disciplining (as you saw in an earlier chapter) and setting boundaries. Praise your toddler or reward them with a toy or fruit when they follow the rules of your boundaries. Assure them that they will get another reward in the future if they keep at it.

Remember, your toddlers may test boundaries repeatedly, but don't become upset. Try to control your emotions and avoid reacting impulsively or with anger, as it can escalate the situation. Furthermore, while consistency is important for setting empowering boundaries, you should be willing to adapt your approach as your child grows. What works for one child may not work for another, so be open to trying different strategies.

Helpful Roadmaps for Routines

Humans are sticklers for routines, and toddlers are no different. Once you have set boundaries for them, establishing a routine is the next natural step. There is one major benefit of a routine among toddlers – research suggests that it helps them sleep better at night. If they are waking up at odd hours, lack of a routine is one of the main reasons.

You may have already developed a set routine as an adult (which may have been disrupted because of your child). However, while establishing your little one's schedule, you should put their needs before your own.

- Take their nap times, meal times, and bedtimes into account.

- Include their essential activities like play times and learning activities.

- Their sleep hours, including daytime naps, are critical additions. Their total sleep time should amount to around 12 hours.

- Incorporate outdoor physical activities like running, jumping, exploring, etc.

- Include games that test them mentally, like puzzles or building blocks.

- Add times for activities that boost their imagination, like nature walks and treasure boxes.
- Be prepared to adjust the routine based on their changing needs.

Ideally, you don't need to communicate the routine you set for your child, mostly because they don't understand time yet. Just try to follow the same schedule every day, like breakfast at 9:00 AM, playing outside until 11:00 AM, having lunch at 1:00 PM, and so on. As they grow older, you can explain it in simple words when they are following the routine.

For instance, you can say that they had breakfast at the same time as yesterday and compliment or reward them with a sweet delicacy. Don't forget to design your own routine based on theirs. You need to prioritize self-care to care for your child.

Here's a sample toddler routine template you can use and adjust according to your little one's schedule:

Morning

- **Wake your toddler up at a set time each morning, around 8:00 AM.**

Morning Routine

- Change their diaper or help them use the potty.
- Brush their teeth with a child-friendly toothbrush and toothpaste.
- Wash their face and hands.
- Get dressed for the day.
- Have a nutritious breakfast together. Encourage them to participate in simple tasks like pouring cereal or spreading peanut butter on toast.
- Let them engage in activities like building blocks, coloring, or playing with toys.

Mid-morning (around 10:00 AM)

- Offer a healthy snack like fruit slices, yogurt, or crackers and cheese.
- Spend time outdoors if possible. Take a walk, visit a playground, or play in your backyard.

Late Morning (around 11:00 AM)

- Read them a book or let them engage in sensory play (e.g., playing with Play-Doh or water play).
- Let them play all on their own while you attend to household tasks or work.

Lunchtime

- Give them a balanced lunch with the right mix of veggies. At times, you can let them choose.
- Encourage them to help clear their plate and clean up any spills or messes.

Afternoon

- If your toddler still naps, establish a consistent naptime routine like reading a book, singing a lullaby, or cuddling before laying them down.
- If they no longer nap, let them relax as they see fit. Encourage activities like looking at picture books, listening to music, or playing quietly in their room.

Late Afternoon (around 4:00 PM)

- It's time for a little snack again.
- If the sun isn't too scorching, spend time outdoors. Let them run, climb, and explore.

Evening

- Enjoy a family dinner together. Listen to them talk about their day.
- Bathe them in warm water and let them play with bath toys in the tub.

Bedtime Routine

- Put on pajamas
- Brush their teeth again
- Read a bedtime story or sing a lullaby
- Tuck your toddler into bed for a good night's sleep

Expert Insights

While you are setting boundaries and routines for your child, they may not understand the reasons behind your efforts. It may lead them to reject your suggestions and go against your set schedule. It is important to remain calm during these situations.

They are children who don't understand much about the world around them. If you become angry or anxious, they may reflect your behavior, and you will end up in a power struggle with them, where you try to explain why they should do something, and they do the exact opposite. You should try to avoid these struggles at all costs. Here are a few expert insights that will help:

- Dr. Laura Markham, a clinical psychologist and parenting expert, emphasizes the importance of consistency in discipline. She suggests that parents need to follow through with consequences every time a boundary is crossed, as this helps toddlers understand the importance of rules and expectations.
- According to Dr. Alan Kazdin, professor of psychology and child psychiatry at Yale University, parents should be clear and firm when setting boundaries for toddlers. Clear communication helps them understand what is expected of them, while firmness conveys the importance of following rules.
- Dr. Becky Bailey, author of "Conscious Discipline," recommends offering toddlers choices within limits to help them feel a sense of autonomy while still respecting boundaries. For example, instead of saying, "Put on your pajamas," you can say, "Do you want to wear the blue pajamas or the red pajamas?"

Remember that parents are natural role models for their children. They will do what you do, only more enthusiastically. For instance, if you are being aggressive toward your partner, your child will be more aggressive toward their friends. Avoid being a negative role model and be more positive, at least when you are around them.

Demonstrate all the qualities that you wish to see in your child, from empathizing with their faults to showing empathy for their mistakes. Make the routine you want them to follow your own. For example, brush your teeth as you brush theirs or play with them during their playtime.

The Innate Connection Between Well-Defined Boundaries and Positive Behavior

Put yourself in your toddler's shoes. Imagine you are your little one. You have come into the world only recently, and you have no idea how it works. You know you can do whatever you want, but not exactly. You may feel the urge to eat anything because you are hungry. Your curiosity about your surroundings may triumph over everything else.

However, out of the blue, your caregivers or your parents say that you need to follow a few rules. You will reject them at first, choosing to do what you want, but you will eventually realize the importance of those rules and boundaries since your parents would explain them to you.

You will understand why it's not right to hit a fellow human being, why it's wrong to eat unripe fruit, and why it feels bad to behave badly with other people. Positive behavior in toddlers stems from well-defined boundaries, which include the right explanations. It's not a system but a way of life.

Chapter 7: Remember: Patience, Consistency, and Love

There is no positive parenting framework without love, patience, and consistency. Love upholds positive parenting and is the motivation behind this approach to raising your child. The rays of patience and consistency emanate from the sun of love. Patience allows you to identify which techniques to apply, and consistency increases their effectiveness.

Positive parenting requires patience and consistency.[16]

Change is gradual by using this parenting framework. The methods of redirection and positive reinforcement work based on the principle of consistency. The little you do daily has lasting impacts. To build a positive environment, it takes one brick at a time. The slow progress of daily repetition creates lasting transformation.

When applying these techniques in the tornado of toddlerhood, your success will not come from copy-paste techniques. Positive parenting is crafted with a focus on individuals. The connection that your love promotes and the engagement your patience cradles are the sockets into which you plug practical methods.

Applying love, consistency, and patience to positive parenting is like an extraction process that draws out the best in your child. Parenting is not a sterile process with a set of laboratory protocols. The learning done in consistent interaction helps you respond to behavior with awareness through invested observation.

You are not a machine. There is no slot to insert a coin that produces patience, consistency, and expressions of love. Therefore, as much as you work with your toddler, you must do the internal labor to grow your capabilities. Toddlers are surprisingly observant. They can pick up on many subtleties you'd expect them to miss. Strengthening a parent-child bond starts with the relationship you have with yourself.

The triangle of love, patience, and consistency reinforces the bridge of connection created by the blueprint of positive parenting. Behavior is social and developmental. There are constant changes you can only detect through a loving connection and the patience to understand. You must be aware of this evolution to respond appropriately with effective parenting techniques. The toddler years are a lot, but they go by quickly. This creates a short window to instill long-lasting life skills in this sensitive period.

Patience

It started with getting ready, then it was the struggle to get them in the car seat, next was the shopping center tantrum, and the fight with the sibling, topped with the struggle of controlling the chaos at dinner time. In any of these moments, a slip in patience could cause a counterproductive response. The mountain of pressure increases when constantly dealing with your lovable gremlins. Sustaining patience in parenting is crucial for facilitating emotional intelligence and acceptable behavior. Learning to cultivate patience is the safety net that keeps you from slipping into outdated modalities like punishments or yelling.

With resilience and a focus on understanding your child, you can overcome the challenges of raising a toddler. The difficult moments are the best opportunities to instill helpful lessons. Without love as the foundation and patience as a core pillar, the positive parenting approach cannot be supported. Navigating rough terrain requires preparation. Your patience can be developed with the right tools. Slowing down to assess and understand situations promotes better responses.

Resilience and Understanding

Parental stress is an overlooked reality. The picture-perfect parenting posted on social media doesn't show how draining it can be. The stress and anxiety associated with raising a toddler create a spiral. Stress impacts a child's behavior, which then adds to the parent's stress in a feedback loop of negativity. Stress management is essential to remain resilient for you and your child. Through breathing exercises and mindfulness, you can bring yourself into the present to understand your child better and build the patience to work through the lava of behavioral issues.

Positive parenting is a long-term process. There is seldom immediate change. Furthermore, practicing the self-control that the approach requires can seem impossible. In episodes of heightened emotions, it does take a lot to maintain a controlled disposition. Raising your toddler is intrinsically tied to how you manipulate your internal alchemy. You need emotional regulation to manage your feelings while acting as a filter for your child to process their experiences. By taking conscious action to carefully curate your communication and behavior and taking stress management measures, you build an effective toolbox for parenting with patience.

Slowing down to a controlled reaction allows you to access the empathy to be patient with your child. These moments of self-control, when you feel like you're about to explode, build your child's life skills. Pattern creation takes time and repetition, and the tedious process can be tiring. Having to constantly go through the same steps while seeing little progress can make you feel trapped. Your patience pays off with the validation of your persistence when you see your toddler's behavioral shifts and unexpected altruism.

Responding to Behavior

Patience isn't about bowing to all your toddler's irrational demands. It is about understanding their motivations, perceptions, and emotions. Toddler emotions are valid. Their experience has all the depth of a fully grown adult. They are reacting to their environment in the only ways they know how. You are assisting in the development of their behavioral and emotional regulation skills. They have not yet learned the manual to operate the machine of social interaction, nor have their legs gotten long enough to reach the pedals.

Think of responding to behavior at the toddler stage, like allowing a child to sit on your lap and play with the steering of a parked car. A young child's frame of reference is exceedingly narrow. You are feeding your child the data to shape their conduct with the world. For lessons to solidify, a toddler needs a constant stream of repetition. Patience for persistently engaging your child with focused attention, especially while they are in distress or misbehaving, is crucial. Once this foundation is established, the techniques of positive parenting become more impactful.

Your emotions are just as valid as your toddler's. Your frustration is understandable and expected. Building a culture of mutual respect takes time. The seeming one-sidedness of interactions with a toddler compounds into a culture. Your patient engagement in carefully teaching your child how to regulate themselves is rewarded with the cognitive ability, emotional intelligence, and problem-solving skills your toddler develops.

Cultivating Patience in Your Home

The patience you exhibit is a model for your toddler. Regulating yourself emotionally with your child during distressing moments significantly contributes to their development. Communicating it in a way they understand helps them internalize it easily. Here are a few practical techniques you can apply to practice and promote patience in the home.

- **Recognize Your Triggers.** Some situations can quickly turn up the heat from a simmer to a full boil. Your emotional state could be stabbed with tantrums, whining, running late, or tiredness. When you identify your triggers, you can prepare to manage them. For example, if you know running late stresses you, you can prepare your clothes the evening before.

- **Self-Care Is Important.** No one can give of themselves eternally without feeling drained. You are more beneficial to your child when you function optimally. Raising a toddler can seem like an endless job, but you must find time to take breaks for self-care. This could be as simple as reading a fifteen-minute book or having a silent glass of wine.

- **Slow Down and Communicate.** Sometimes, working through your patience comes with understanding. Asking your toddler questions and observing their body language could provide insight into what is disturbing them. You can be a support and help them work through it.

- **Practice Mindfulness.** Bringing yourself into the present moment can eradicate anxiety. You can pause to analyze a scenario practically by using your breath to make your next step impactful. In a heightened moment, taking five to ten deep breaths to root yourself into the moment can help you explore positive options.

Consistency

Structure promotes growth. Your toddler's limited lens of the world is like you being dropped in a foreign country, not speaking the language without a map. To find their footing on these unstable grounds, they rely on you for explanations. Can you recall what you did at 10 a.m. on March 7? Unless this is a significant day, like a birthday or anniversary, the answer is likely no. The lessons you have learned came through experiences and repetitions. Before you could read, you recited the alphabet every day in a classroom. Similarly, a toddler's behavioral map is drawn with routine and expectations.

With predictable responses, a toddler can find their role and participate, creating a sense of independence. They can learn to solve problems by applying appropriate behaviors in overlapping contexts. For example, a child who does not climb on the benches at home will likely not do it in a church. Predictable environments and responses allow a child to exist comfortably. The security of knowing what will happen creates room for controlled self-expression.

Routines, Rules, and Expectations

It's tempting to give up on routine or to bend the rules, especially when your child is not cooperating. The consistency of applied rules positively contributes to your child's development. Routines create clear expectations. Dinner is not in the kitchen one night, and then another evening, it's in the dining room. For a child who is still processing social conventions, it makes it unclear what dinner is and what is expected when sitting down to eat. The predictability that repetition fosters is the security a child needs to make sense of the world.

Being able to anticipate what is about to happen grows confidence in a toddler. When their predictions are proven right, they develop trust in their independent assessments. Rules create the boundaries of what your child is allowed to explore and how they can express their interactions with the world. Consistency in rules means that the boundary cannot be moved regardless of your child's reaction. If you said they can't have candy after 5 p.m., then that is the law. You can help them process their reaction but at no point can you give into them.

When you enforce the rule sometimes and slack on occasion, giving into the boundary-crossing demand, it creates unstable confusion. A toddler can have an aggravated emotional experience because they cannot understand why it was okay yesterday, but today, it's banned. Inconsistency creates shaky ground on which to build their understanding. When you apply boundaries inconsistently, a toddler will not link their limitations to their behavior but will begin to internalize it as an issue with themselves, which can later create insecurities.

Consequences of Inconsistent Parenting

There are many ways of parenting inconsistently. A parent set irregular boundaries by being overly permissible with her three-year-old. Her child would erupt into temper tantrums when they didn't get their way. She would attempt to enforce a rule but would tire and eventually give in. This parent was driven by the desire to end her child's distress. However, she missed the core of the problem, which was emotions. She started holding firm boundaries but helping her child through negative emotions with empathy and understanding.

Melissa often defaulted to shouting at her four-year-old boy. She realized that this was the fastest way to get him to listen. She would try using calmer methods but would shortly escalate to yelling. The high-energy boy wasn't shy and would often speak to strangers in public. When visiting people, he would go into their rooms and fiddle with gadgets. Melissa repetitively applied shouting as a mechanism of behavioral control.

Her son's curiosity was unfulfilled because he was not taught what he could do but was yelled at for what he couldn't do. Melissa learned that her son was not misbehaving but had misdirected energy. She began setting up a daily routine that catered to his nature. She also made sure that she planned activities to keep the energetic son engaged when they went places. By regularly following their vibrant and interactive routine, Melissa was able to manage her son's behavior better.

Inconsistency births erratic behavior and emotional outbursts. Your toddler does not have a fully developed conception of what behavioral control is. Therefore, clarity is essential. It's like learning a new language. Your teacher would need to speak slowly, pronouncing the sound of syllables. They would also need to repeat the words often so you could memorize them. In practice, you will say many of the sentences wrong sometimes, making outrageous statements. Your teacher would correct you, understanding that you are a beginner. Similarly, your toddler needs to be reminded how to self-regulate repeatedly.

Positive Reinforcement Strategies

Positive reinforcement is the driver of behavioral correction in positive parenting. You validate desirable actions when you cheer or give them a high five. These signs of affection create positive ties to welcomed patterns. Here are a few positive reinforcement techniques you may find helpful.

- **Physical Affection.** Touch is one of the most powerful connections humans share. Whether it is a handshake at a business meeting or a hug you give a family member you haven't seen in a while, touch means something. When you notice your toddler behaving well, immediately provide affection with a congratulatory high-five or an affirming hug. For touch to be effective, you must implement it repeatedly for similar behaviors so that your toddler establishes the mental connection.

- **Touch for Emotional Support.** Consistency with your boundaries means that your toddler will sometimes be upset, frustrated, or disappointed. Acknowledging their emotions while staying firm in your boundaries shows empathy and builds a strong parent-child bond. Using an affirming hug to guide your child through the trauma of rejection or disappointment is essential to developing emotional well-being.

- **Verbal Praise.** Continually praise your child for accomplishments and good behavior. This validation and affirmation make a toddler feel empowered. Communication is multilayered. Couple your praise with an upbeat tone, cheers, engaging body language, and eye contact.

- **Make It Communal.** Children are keen to integrate into a group. Their biological drive compels them to develop a group identity alongside their individuality. Telling another adult about their positive actions in their presence builds confidence.

Love

Out of the positive parenting tenets of patience, love, and consistency – love stands as the most important. From the control center of love, consistency, and patience are distributed. Love is not only felt; it is *demonstrated*. You undeniably love your toddler. Channeling this love in ways that attract the best outcomes is the *magic* of positive parenting. Transforming love from emotional to practical application creates the warmth that nourishes a child's wellbeing.

Love is a complex, multifaceted experience. One of the core elements of parental love is wanting the best for your child. This intention shapes your decision-making. Therefore, the positive parenting framework integrates love into its fundamental principles. With love as the motivator and a stable frame to deliver your love to your toddler in a consumable way, you will establish a powerful bond with your child.

Facets of Love in Parenting

With techniques like positive reinforcement, it is easy to slip into thinking love is conditional. However, your toddler has to experience the rawest and purest forms of love from you. Knowing that you care about them and are there to support them emotionally is crucial to their development. Affection should be freely shared, and quality time should be taken seriously. By using focused attention, you can exhibit the unconditional love your toddler deserves and needs in order to thrive.

Your child needs ample positive affirmations to develop high self-esteem and the confidence to excel.[17]

Your child needs ample positive affirmations to develop high self-esteem and the confidence to excel. These uplifting messages delivered in love encourage pushing your child further. Sometimes, you can see your child is holding back from an experience they will likely enjoy. Simply by reassuring them, you can stimulate the confidence to take that step into the unknown that brings overflowing satisfaction.

Your child's emotional development is directly joined to kindness and affection. Emotional intelligence is the ability to understand your own emotions and interpret the feelings of others so that you can shape your behavior. A safe environment with boundless affection creates security for children to investigate their emotions while observing yours. In this way, their emotional development is accelerated by immersed interaction.

Expressing Love Daily

Toddlers are open and receiving of all the love you have to give. Their affectionate nature is heartwarming. There are numerous ways you can introduce healthy displays of love into your relationship with your child.

- **Verbal Affirmations.** These are words of encouragement, cheers, praise, and expressions of gratitude. Your toddler's verbal skills are quickly developing. The words you use need consideration to create an environment of love that facilitates respect. Maintaining an uplifting demeanor creates comfort for your toddler to express themself freely.

- **Non-verbal displays of Love.** Hug, cuddle, pat, and high-five your child often. People crave human connection. A child is adjusting to experiencing the world through their vibrant senses. With touch, you reinforce your support for them. Touch, like a comforting hug, can be used for comfort during difficult experiences or to highlight positive progress with a pat on the back when a toddler puts their shoes on correctly.

- **Spending Quality Time.** Your ability to respond to your child's behavior and feelings is unfolded in the time you spend with them. Put down your phone and pause the multitasking to give your child undivided attention. These moments strengthen your bond with your child.

- **Positive Reinforcement.** When you spend enough time with your toddler, you'll realize that there are tons of noteworthy things they do daily. As you lovingly interact with them, notice their kind gestures and selflessness. When you notice these qualities, reaffirm your child with verbal encouragement or physical affection. You can say something like, "It makes me feel great when you share your toys with me. Thank you so much."

Guidance Through Mistakes and Misbehavior

The unexpected wonders of toddler misbehavior can be extremely trying. It can be excruciatingly hard to ensure that your love comes through in your interactions at these moments. Correction is more impactful when delivered with love. Love creates understanding, which builds the patience to work through your child's thoughts, feelings, and behavior. Correction requires empathy to see the underlying motivators of action in the positive parenting system.

As you open your perception to understand your child, a new world is unveiled. You realize that there is a multiplicity of ways to exist, and your child is exploring a unique one. This living understanding underpins how you can positively discipline your child while motivating their emotional well-being.

Patience is the garnish of love. Being slow to anger and quick to forgive helps your child know that you are a safe space. Your control communicates that you are a pillar your child can lean on in their uncertainty. Raising a toddler is not an easy task, but being one isn't a breeze either. Only through patience can you comprehend your child's needs and desires. Taking the time to explore your child's mind enhances the lessons you can teach because you meet them at their level.

Love is the ocean from which the rivers of patience and consistency extend. These pillars are interconnected, working together for the benefit of your child. The lessons you learn when you are first exploring what it means to be a human are deeply ingrained. The toddler years are like a child's running start toward their life trajectory.

Love, patience, and consistency are the best ways to prepare them for a brighter future. These principles, applied through positive parenting, create emotional well-being, social skills, and confidence that will follow your child into adulthood. Developing healthy relationships in adulthood is often reflected in the parent-child bond someone had growing up.

Positive parenting is not cold and lifeless. It is a breathing approach that is filled with emotional understanding and mutual respect. Building the structures that support these values takes time. Through consistency, you can create a culture in the home that mediates your toddler's behavior and emotions in a way that is fulfilling to them while allowing them to learn.

Chapter 8: Managing Challenges and Staying Calm

Have you ever been in a situation where your toddler throws a tantrum in the middle of the grocery store because you won't buy them that shiny toy they just spotted? It feels like the whole world is watching, and you're left feeling frustrated and embarrassed. But guess what? You're not alone. Toddler tantrums are like a rite of passage in parenthood – almost every parent has been there.

There are several ways to manage the challenges that come with having a toddler while staying calm.[18]

Tantrums, as common as they are, don't have to be your forever reality. There are ways to tame them and help your child understand and express their emotions in healthier ways. Have you ever envied those parents whose kids seem to listen to every word they say, who behave like little angels even in the midst of chaos? It's natural to wonder, "How do they do it?" especially when your own child seems to transform into a tiny tornado at the slightest inconvenience. Well, take heart. It's not as impossible as it might seem to turn your tantrum-thrower into one of those well-behaved wonders.

This chapter will help you do exactly that; however, you will have to change your mindset when it comes to tantrums. You need to understand why they happen and, more importantly, how to stop them from happening so often. There are different types of tantrums and meltdowns, and knowing how to deal with them will get you out of a lot of tough situations. Positive parenting can make a real difference – not just in the heat of the moment, but for the long haul.

Why Do They Lose Control?

Aggressive behavior in children might seem like a serious problem at first glance. However, in many cases, children are simply reacting impulsively because they haven't yet learned to control their actions. This is particularly true for younger children, from birth until around 18 months old, when they're still figuring out how to express complex feelings like loneliness, helplessness, fear, or confusion.

Despite the worries you may have about your child's aggressive or irritable behavior, you should recognize that this is a normal stage of development that every child goes through. As they grow and mature in an environment with clear boundaries and consistent discipline, their aggressive tendencies naturally begin to diminish. You can still manage the behavior by utilizing specific behavioral techniques. First, explore the different types of unruly behavior your toddler may exhibit:

Tantrums

This is what a tantrum can look like (not that you need a picture of how tantrums go): your little one is peacefully playing with their toys one moment, and the next, they're on the floor kicking, screaming, and maybe even banging their head. These outbursts can last anywhere from a few seconds to a couple of minutes, with the peak intensity hitting right at the start. And it's not uncommon for them to happen daily, especially in kids under four.

Tantrums aren't just attention-seeking antics with toddlers.[19]

However, unlike what many people believe, tantrums aren't just attention-seeking antics. They're often the only way toddlers know how to express big emotions like frustration or anger. Imagine trying to put together a puzzle but not having the right pieces. That's how it feels for them when they can't get what they want or do something they're struggling with.

The good news? For most kids, tantrums eventually fade away as they learn better ways to cope with their emotions. It's part of growing up and figuring out how to navigate the rollercoaster of feelings that come with change. However, suppose tantrums persist past the age of four. In that case, it might be a sign that something deeper is going on, like trouble learning or difficulties in making friends at daycare or play school.

Stubbornness

Dealing with a stubborn toddler can sometimes feel like hitting a brick wall. From the moment they start toddling around, they're on a mission to do everything themselves, without any help from the grown-ups. This can sometimes leave adults feeling a bit frazzled and rushed. However, when you try to push back against their stubbornness, it often just makes things worse.

So, what's the solution? Instead of butting heads with your little one, you need to teach them the power of cooperation. Although learning to cooperate isn't always easy, they will eventually understand the concept. That's why it's better to show them rather than just tell them why working together is good for them.

For example, if you're cleaning the house, invite your toddler to join in. At first, they might resist, but as they pitch in and see how much faster and easier things get done when you work as a team, they start to get it.

Shyness

Every child is unique, with their own way of approaching the big wide world of social interactions. Some kids dive right into new situations, talking to strangers like old friends. Others prefer to stick close to the familiar, finding comfort in the company of those they already know.

Neither approach is better or worse than the other; they're just different ways that kids navigate the world around them. As parents, you're often bombarded with advice from experts and well-meaning friends, but you should remember that you know your little one the best. There's no one-size-fits-all solution to parenting, especially when it comes to supporting a shy child. Sure, you want your baby to grow up happy, strong, and respectful. But sometimes, despite your best efforts, things don't go according to plan.

Aggressiveness

Aggressiveness in toddlers can be unexpected and intense, and it can leave you feeling overwhelmed and unsure of how to handle it. Your little one might resort to physical aggression, like hitting or biting, especially when they're feeling frustrated or unable to express themselves verbally. Sharing isn't always second nature to toddlers, and they might use aggression to assert their dominance over toys or objects they desire. Sometimes, toddlers even resort to pushing or shoving when they're feeling overwhelmed or seeking attention.

In this case, encourage your child to use words to express their feelings instead of resorting to aggression. For example, teach them to say, "I'm angry" instead of hitting or biting. Children learn by example, so make sure to model calm and gentle behavior even in the face of frustration. Show them how to take deep breaths or walk away from a situation that's upsetting them.

Establish clear rules about acceptable behavior and consequences for aggression. Consistency is key here, so make sure to enforce these boundaries consistently. Talk about your toddler's feelings and validate their experiences to help them understand and label their emotions. Let them know that it's okay to feel angry or frustrated, but it's not okay to hurt others.

Meltdowns

Crying fits are a common form of meltdown – often triggered by frustration, fatigue, or even hunger. Ever been in a crowded store when your toddler decides it's the perfect time to unleash ear-piercing screams? That's another classic meltdown scenario, which is fueled by overstimulation or feeling overwhelmed. It's like they're auditioning for a role in a dramatic movie – maybe your toddler dramatically flops on the floor, kicking and flailing as if the world is ending. These floor flops are a hallmark of meltdowns, signaling intense emotions and a loss of control.

What can you do? Let your toddler know that it's okay to feel big emotions like anger or sadness. Sometimes, giving your toddler a sense of control can help defuse a meltdown. Offer simple choices like "Do you want the red cup or the blue cup?" to help them feel empowered. A change of scenery or a fun distraction can help shift your toddler's focus away from whatever triggered the meltdown. Try singing a silly song, playing a game, or offering a favorite toy to help calm them down.

Keep Calm and Take a Deep Breath

When your toddler launches into a full-blown tantrum, it can feel like you're stuck in a tornado with no clear way out. You may find yourself grasping at straws, trying anything and everything to make it stop. Maybe you're tempted to give in to your child's demands, or perhaps you're convinced that a quick time-out will nip the tantrum in the bud. It's a desperate scramble to regain control before the situation spirals out of hand.

Surprisingly, stopping a tantrum isn't as impossible as it may seem. Contrary to popular belief, toddlers aren't just being difficult on purpose – they're struggling to understand and regulate their emotions. Believe it or not, you can help them recognize what's happening, why it's a problem, and how to overcome it. How? Breathing.

Think about it – when you're overwhelmed with emotions, what's the first thing you do to regain composure? Most likely, you take a deep breath. Biologically speaking, deep breathing triggers a response in your body, activating the vagus nerve, which regulates your heart rate and promotes relaxation.

Toddlers can learn this, too. While they might not understand the concept of taking a big breath, you can guide them through it using playful techniques. You can encourage them to take deep breaths during playtime and help them learn to associate deep breathing with calming down. Over time, they'll develop the ability to self-soothe and prevent tantrums before they even start.

So, how do you trigger your child to breathe deeply and calm down? Here are some simple techniques to try:

Visualizing

A favorite method among children for practicing deep breathing involves using visualization and pretend play. You can engage your child by asking them to imagine sniffing a fragrant flower and then blowing out a pretend candle held by you. This simple activity encourages your child to pause and take deep breaths, promoting a sense of calmness. For added effectiveness, choose a flower scent your child enjoys and pretend to hold a big birthday cake candle for them to blow out.

Belly Breathing

This technique focuses on guiding your child to breathe from their diaphragm rather than their chest, which can often happen when they're stressed. Have your child lie on their back and place a stuffed animal or a small rock on their stomach. Encourage them to take deep breaths, watching as the object rises and falls with each breath. Not only does this help your child regulate their breathing, but it also serves as a distraction, shifting their focus to the movement of the object.

Feather Play

Gather feathers from down pillows or jackets or purchase craft feathers from the store. Encourage your child to blow the feathers into the air, watching as they float and move around. This playful activity not only promotes deep breathing but also provides an engaging distraction. Experiment with feathers of different shapes and sizes, turning it into a fun game to see which feather flies the farthest.

Dragon Breaths

When your child is feeling angry or frustrated, guide them to release their emotions through "dragon breaths." Have them take a big, deep breath, lift their head to the sky, and exhale forcefully, imagining they're breathing out their anger like a dragon breathing fire. This technique not only encourages deep breathing but also helps your child release pent-up emotions in a constructive way.

One Hug a Day Keeps the Tantrum Away

Your child craves attention – that's just part of being a kid. They need that connection with you to feel safe and loved, and one of the best ways to give it to them is through hugs, cuddles, and affection. When your child is in the midst of a tantrum, sometimes what they really need is a big dose of love. Try soothing them with hugs and cuddles, but also respect their boundaries while still offering comfort.

Once the storm has passed and your child is calm, you should also remember to give them mindful hugs regularly. This ensures they get the affection and care they need at the moment, preventing future tantrums and building a strong bond between them. When you hug your child, both of you release oxytocin, the "love hormone," which naturally reduces stress. Regular hugs help your child learn to self-regulate and trust that they can always turn to you for comfort.

Incorporating mindful hugging into your routine can make a world of difference. Offer hugs mid-tantrum, teaching your child that they can rely on hugs to feel better and cope with the world around them. This can lead to fewer and easier-to-manage tantrums overall. Mindful hugging means giving your full attention to the embrace and holding your child close for longer than a quick squeeze. It's a powerful moment that lights up rewarding areas in both of your brains. Make hugs a regular part of your day, and never use them as punishment or to withhold affection.

If your child is verbal, ask them how the hug makes them feel. Pay attention to their response and adjust your approach accordingly. Remember these tips: hug with your whole body and awareness, hug regularly, eliminate distractions, and offer hugs during moments of overwhelm or frustration.

Avoid Punishment

Positive parenting means understanding your child – their behavior and their feelings. It's about digging deeper to uncover the root cause behind their actions and offering alternatives to negative behavior. When kids act out, adults often only see the surface – what needs correcting or the symptom of a deeper issue. It's up to you to explain the consequences of their actions, whether it's a natural outcome like feeling cold because they refuse a sweater or a logical one like being late to a party because they didn't leave on time.

Positive parenting involves setting clear expectations with a calm tone and explaining the consequences of not meeting them. It creates a space for learning without guilt or fear of punishment. Children learn through trial and error, with parents guiding them along the way. It's a journey of attempts and mistakes until they master new skills. Your role is to provide direction and patience as their teachers. Remember that children's brains are still developing, and immature behavior is normal for their age. No matter how you feel as a parent, you can't change this scientific fact.

Parenting requires repetition and patience, both for you and your children. Some days, it may feel like you're saying the same thing repeatedly, but that's all part of the journey. Children learn about the world and social norms from their parents. It's not just about acquiring knowledge; it's about learning how to navigate society and its rules. Therefore, setting boundaries is crucial for children's development. Children are capable problem solvers if given the chance. Instead of jumping in with criticism, you should give them space to find solutions themselves.

Listening to children is powerful – it helps them think clearly and find solutions to their problems. While using fear and control may work in the short term, they can hinder a child's development in the long run. Positive reinforcement and support build confidence and encourage positive behavior. Teaching children to understand their thoughts and emotions is essential for healthy relationships and problem-solving.

Discipline isn't about punishment – it's about supporting children's self-discipline and helping them learn from their mistakes. How can you do this? Here are a few techniques to get you started:

Stay Calm

Instead of yelling, try speaking calmly to your child. When you use a calm voice, it shows them that you're patient and understanding. How you react affects how they behave. Positive parenting is important for building a strong, healthy relationship with your child. For example, when your child spills their drink, instead of getting angry, you can calmly say, "It's okay; accidents happen. Let's clean it up together." This approach helps them learn that mistakes are normal and that you're there to help them.

Take a Break

Taking a break is important because being patient takes time. It can be tough to figure out why your child acts in a certain way and what you can do to support them. When you're busy and your child needs something, patience can feel even harder, but patience is all about understanding your child's needs and feelings. For instance, if your child is having a tantrum because they want a toy, taking a moment to breathe and understand their frustration can help you respond calmly and effectively. So, giving yourself a break allows you to recharge and approach situations with more patience and understanding.

Be Empathetic

Understanding your child is key to positive parenting. It shapes how you communicate and show respect. It's natural to feel frustrated when you don't understand why your child acts in a certain way. Toddlers can be nervous, tearful, or loud, and it's easy to lose patience. But, as a parent, you have unconditional love for your child. By approaching conversations with them from a place of love, you'll start to understand them better and find it easier to be patient. For example, if your child is throwing a tantrum, instead of getting upset, try to understand what they're feeling and why. This empathy helps you respond with patience and support.

Encourage Independence

Encouraging your child to be independent is a great way to practice patience. Instead of doing everything for them, give them the chance to complete tasks on their own. This helps them develop independence while also teaching you to be patient. For instance, if your child is struggling to tie their shoes, resist the urge to step in and do it for them. Instead, give them the time and space to figure it out themselves. This not only builds their confidence but also allows you to practice patience as they learn and grow.

Relax

Discovering ways to quickly calm yourself down is crucial for building patience. There are simple techniques you can try, like deep breathing or counting to ten. You might also find relaxation in activities like baking a cake or going for a short walk. Knowing what works best for you can help you regain composure and approach situations with a calmer mindset. For instance, if you feel yourself getting frustrated with your child's behavior, taking a few deep breaths or stepping away for a moment can help you stay patient and composed.

Toddler Discipline

Navigating discipline as a parent, especially if you're new to it, can be quite the puzzle. Everyone wants to raise well-behaved kids who can handle life's ups and downs with grace. Luckily, there's no one-size-fits-all approach except for those that leave lasting scars. The key is finding what works best for your child's unique personality and behavior.

Praise and Encouragement

The use of positive words and acknowledging good behavior can work wonders. Whether it's a high five or a simple "good job," kids love praise and will often strive to earn more of it.

Reframe Your Approach

Instead of focusing on what they shouldn't do, try framing instructions in a positive light. For instance, instead of saying, "Don't run," try, "Let's walk, please." It's all about encouraging positive behavior rather than just avoiding the negative.

Ignore Tantrums

Sometimes, the best response to a tantrum is no response at all. Ignoring the behavior sends a clear message that it won't get them what they want. It may seem tough, but staying calm and not giving in is key.

Time-Outs

A classic technique, time-outs give kids a chance to cool off and reflect on their actions. Choose a quiet spot for them to take a break, making sure it's safe and visible to you. Keep the time short and use it as an opportunity to discuss what happened afterward.

Distraction

When you see trouble brewing, steer your child's attention elsewhere. Offer a new toy or activity to shift their focus away from whatever is causing the problem. It's a simple but effective way to redirect their energy.

Redirection

During a tantrum, your child's emotional brain is in control, making rational thinking difficult. Redirection can help bring their logical side back to the surface. You can redirect attention by showing or offering something new to distract them. Even toddlers benefit from this technique. For instance, if your child throws blocks in frustration, calmly suggest a different activity, like playing with cars or going outside to throw a ball. The goal isn't to scold or punish but to guide your child toward more positive behaviors. By gently redirecting their attention, you're helping them learn to cope with their emotions in a healthier way.

When your child throws a tantrum, it's natural to feel stressed out. That immediate urge to make them stop crying is hardwired into your biology. But remember, being upset doesn't justify losing your temper.

So, make sure you stay calm.

Before jumping into action, take a moment to breathe. Deep breaths can clear your head and prevent you from reacting impulsively. Instead of getting frustrated, try to empathize. Your child isn't trying to make your life difficult; they're struggling with big emotions. They need your support, not judgment. Tantrums happen, especially in public. Remember, other parents understand what you're going through. Don't let judgmental stares or comments get to you. Stay focused on helping your child.

Chapter 9: Raising a Happy Child

As you reach the end of this book, it's safe to say that you gained insights into the numerous aspects of positive parenting. You also understand how to connect with your child, look out for their well-being, and build a healthy relationship with them, all while fostering their independence and encouraging them to become self-sufficient. From learning to communicate positively with your child to understanding how you can navigate all the stress and overwhelm that comes with being a parent, this book offers invaluable insights into navigating the thrilling yet challenging rollercoaster of raising a toddler. This final chapter integrates all the core principles and knowledge provided in this book to enhance your child's development and well-being and ensure their happiness.

Raising a happy toddler is a parent's ultimate goal.[20]

Positive Parenting

Positive parenting is all about creating a supportive and compassionate environment where children are encouraged to express themselves, learn, and grow. This type of parenting improves a child's mental, emotional, and social well-being while still ensuring that they are mannered and disciplined. In essence, parents who create positive environments for their children don't only care about instilling rules and correcting their children's mistakes but also desire to build strong relationships with them where there is mutual trust, love, and effective communication.

Creating a positive environment for your child requires you to actively listen to them and validate and empathize with their thoughts, feelings, and experiences. You want your child to be able to tell you everything, whether it's a new idea they have or a problem they're in, without fearing that they'll be judged or misunderstood. This increases your child's sense of security, which is crucial for their emotional health in the long run.

Positive parenting aims to set children up for success in their futures by leaving room for independence and encouraging them to become self-sufficient. That said, parents still look out for their children's well-being and set consistent boundaries. The key is to find the ideal balance between offering guidance without enforcing their opinions when unnecessary and giving children the opportunity to learn from their mistakes and experiences. When you set reasonable expectations and consequences for your child's age, they develop a sense of responsibility and learn to discipline themselves.

Positive parenting also naturally enhances your child's self-esteem and boosts their confidence. It requires you to gently correct their mistakes and show that you're proud of their accomplishments, regardless of how small they are, and good traits. Another crucial aspect of positive parenting is recognizing signs that your child is struggling to avoid adding to their challenge and stress. Offer support during this tough period. By teaching your child to view themselves in a positive light, even when they make mistakes, they develop confidence and a healthy self-image, which allows them to navigate life's challenges with ease and resilience. They trust that they'll be able to make it out of whichever situation they're in. Despite the lenient and all-positive approach of this parenting method, children still end up being disciplined.

You can still practice behavior management without using punitive tactics. This can be achieved by encouraging your child to solve the problems at hand, teaching them to resolve their conflicts, and using positive reinforcement. You can lead your child toward the right answers or behaviors and encourage the ones you want to see more of instead of punishing them. Punishment not only negatively affects a child's overall well-being, but it might also be encountered with resistance and stubbornness.

Positive Discipline

To implement a positive discipline tactic, you need to guide your children's behavior through both empathetic and proactive approaches. This ensures that children are empowered to make good choices as they experience thriving social, emotional, and cognitive development. When implementing positive discipline techniques, you need to set clear boundaries and expectations for your child. Make sure that your daily routines, expectations, and rules are consistent. This helps create a sense of predictability and safety, giving your child a clearer idea of the things that they should and shouldn't do.

Correcting your child's mistakes and misbehaviors isn't enough to get them to adopt better habits. Positive reinforcement, which is all about rewarding positive behaviors, efforts, and accomplishments, either through praise or other incentives, can encourage them to repeat desirable actions and make good choices. Positive discipline also incorporates the use of redirection techniques. If your child engages in undesirable behavior, such as making a huge mess, you can redirect their attention instead of punishing them. Guide them toward better alternatives, making sure you stay collected yet assertive as you do so.

Every action has a reaction. Instead of inflicting the consequences yourself, allow your child to learn from the natural consequences of their behaviors as long as it's safe to do so. For instance, if your child refuses to wear a jacket and it's cold outside, don't force them to wear it and let them experience the cold themselves. They'll likely ask for the jacket in a few minutes. Positive discipline emphasizes the importance of encouraging the development of skills like problem-solving and empathy in children. Lead them toward the exploration of various perspectives and creative thinking about solutions. Most importantly, positive discipline requires you to model the behaviors you wish to see in your child. Your child refers to you regarding how they should interact with the world around them.

Emotional Regulation and Intelligence

As a parent, you need to teach your child how to regulate their emotions and develop emotional intelligence. This allows them to understand how they feel in order to respond to and handle intense emotions effectively. Help them develop the vocabulary they need to voice their feelings and validate their emotions whenever they express them. Dismissing their feelings, no matter how trivial they might seem to you, makes them feel frustrated and misunderstood.

Model empathy by understanding their feelings or encouraging this behavior through storytelling or role-playing, explaining that this is needed for building healthy relationships. Encourage your child to consider other people's perspectives, thoughts, and feelings. It also helps to teach them strategies, such as mindfulness and deep breathing techniques, to manage their emotions and practice self-control. Creating a safe environment for your child to freely discuss their emotions without fearing that they might be judged or criticized helps with emotional regulation and enhances self-esteem and communication skills.

Normalize expressing your emotions to your child. Don't burden them with negative emotions or your problems, but rather share your experiences and how certain situations made you feel with them. Express your emotions in respectful and effective ways, even when you're experiencing negative emotions or are in a difficult situation. Modeling effective self-expression and self-regulation gives your child insight into how to do the same.

Explain that all emotions are valid and respected instead of discouraging them from expressing their frustration, anger, or sadness. Learning to suppress their emotions early on hinders their emotional development and exploration. Building up negative emotions also hinders their ability to communicate with others, which might put a strain on their relationships. Pent-up emotions can also lead to mental and emotional problems. Give your child opportunities where they can safely and constructively express their emotions by maintaining open lines of communication, introducing them to journaling, and engaging them in creative activities.

Effective Communication

Create a culture of effective communication within your family to build mutual trust and a sense of belonging, understanding, and respect. Practice active listening by directing your full attention to your child. Avoid jumping to conclusions regarding what they have to say or interrupting them as they speak. Don't rush to correct your toddler or criticize their mistakes whenever they're talking to you, as this will discourage them from sharing things with you in the future. Show them that you're listening attentively and that you're interested in what they have to say to convey that you value their thoughts, feelings, and experiences.

You should stay respectful toward your child, even in moments of disagreement or whenever you want to correct them. Don't belittle them, use sarcasm, or dismiss their thoughts and feelings. Instead, maintain an empathetic approach and create an accepting atmosphere. Offer guidance whenever needed instead of imposing your own opinions on them. It helps to guide your child toward the right answers or solutions. Setting clear communication expectations allows them to understand the language and listening boundaries you set.

Healthy and Strong Boundaries

Establishing healthy and strong boundaries within your family ensures that all members feel secure and stable. It is the key to fostering mutual respect and the collective emotional, mental, social, and physical well-being of the family. Start by developing clear and concise boundaries that help your child understand their roles and their limits when interacting with each family member. Make sure that the boundaries you set are consistent, apply to everyone, and align with your values to avoid confusion. Cover different areas within family dynamics, such as communication, safety, interaction, respect, and responsibility.

Boundaries are inefficient if you can't communicate them effectively. Make sure to gently and clearly explain the rules and limits to your child. It also helps to explain the rationale behind them and the consequences that follow once these boundaries are overstepped. This way, your child won't feel like these boundaries are imposed on them, thus avoiding feelings of resentment. Encourage your child to share their thoughts and feelings regarding these boundaries and respond to them with rationale.

Find the right balance between establishing boundaries and routines to achieve a sense of structure and leave room for flexibility to accommodate everyone's unique needs and changing circumstances. You should know when to keep the boundaries strict and when to introduce some leniency to make difficult situations and transitions easier for your child. When setting boundaries, keep in mind that you should set realistic expectations that align with your child's age and needs. Don't expect too much from them so that they won't feel pressured and unachieved, nor too little that they think you're treating them like a baby. As they grow older, give them more input in setting boundaries and routines.

Stress Management and Self-Care

Many parents forget that they must look out for their well-being before catering to their children's needs. Being a parent is a full-time job that requires nearly all your strength and energy. You can't do this job efficiently if you don't recharge your power. A vehicle can't drive its passengers anywhere if it runs out of fuel. Recognize signs of stress just as they start to show instead of waiting until you're completely burned out. Stress might manifest as irritability, headaches, tiredness, mood swings, or muscle tension.

You need to put self-care as a priority if you're going to have a balanced life with your toddler.[21]

Prioritizing your self-care is not selfish, even when you have a family to look out for. Putting your own needs before everyone else's allows you to maintain your overall well-being and carry on with your responsibilities. Take the time to engage in relaxing activities, exercise, or hobbies. Don't hesitate to seek support from your friends, family, or even mental health professionals if you need it. Reaching out to your support network will widen your horizons to solve problems more easily and gain insights into different perspectives, help you manage your stress, and allow you to navigate your parental challenges more easily.

Setting realistic expectations for yourself and your children will remove any unnecessary stress and pressure. Perfection can't be achieved on either side, so make sure to cut both of you some slack. As a parent, you'll achieve some great successes and encounter distressing failures. Be sure to approach all situations with self-compassion and flexibility. Practicing mindfulness and learning to live in the present moment without judgment or criticism can enhance your overall health, boost relaxation, aid with emotional regulation, and lower anxiety levels. Spend time in nature, meditate, exercise, practice deep breathing, or do yoga to be more mindful.

Learn to manage your time effectively to increase productivity and efficiency and reduce feelings of being overwhelmed. Know which tasks to prioritize, put off, or discard entirely. It helps to break down your tasks into manageable steps to fit them seamlessly into your routine and other obligations. Maintaining healthy boundaries with your friends, family, and co-workers is crucial to your well-being and allows you to find the balance between different areas in your life. Finally, practicing self-care models this behavior for children. Your child will grow up understanding the importance of prioritizing their mental, emotional, and physical health and needs.

Principles and Reflections

The following are some key principles you can take away from the previous chapters:

- **Exhibit Unconditional Love:** A child should never think that their parents' love and overall approval depend on how well they're doing in life. Don't withhold affection or change the way you treat your child just because they made a mistake. Children should feel certain that they can turn to their parents for love and support whenever they need it. This boosts their sense of security and general well-being.

- **Leave Some Room for Autonomy:** While you should always guide your children toward the right path, especially when they're still young, you should leave some room for independence. Encourage your children to solve their problems, make decisions and choices, and learn from their mistakes while still supporting them and providing facts along the way when needed.

- **Work on Your Emotional Intelligence:** Grow your self-awareness and self-regulation to practice positive parenting effectively. This parenting style also requires you to be empathetic and an effective communicator. Not only does this help you raise your child effectively, but it also allows you to model desirable behaviors to your child.

- **Encourage Your Child's Development:** Make sure to recognize your child's achievements and development in different areas of their life, celebrating their strengths and talents along the way. Offer them opportunities to capitalize on their abilities, practice their hobbies and talents, and practice self-discovery.

- **Be Open to Growth and Learning:** Just like children, parents are on a never-ending journey for growth and learning. Dedicate enough time to improve in the personal and parental aspects of your life, embark on a journey of personal growth, and reflect on your progress and experiences occasionally.

- **Practice Resilience:** Being a parent comes with numerous challenges and obstacles, and so does being a child. Work together with your child on techniques and activities that can help you manage your stress and increase your resilience, such as mindfulness, grounding, breathwork, and meditation. Doing these activities together can also serve as a great bonding experience.

To reflect on your journey so far, you can answer the following questions:

- What are some of the most memorable and joyful moments you have experienced as a parent so far?

- What did being a parent teach you about yourself, and what did you discover about your child in the process?

- Which challenges did you face throughout your parenting journey? How did you overcome them or plan on overcoming them?

- In which ways did you exhibit your love, empathy, and patience toward your child?

- How do you plan on exhibiting your love, empathy, and patience toward your child more effectively in the future?

- What did you do to encourage your child's independence, growth, and development?

- How do you think you've become a better or more capable parent?
- Which goals do you have for yourself and your family?
- How can you create and maintain a supportive environment for your child?
- Which values and principles guide your journey and approach as a parent?

Additional Tips For Nurturing Your Child

- **Learn More about Toddlers' Social and Emotional Development:** Understanding a toddler's developmental stages allows you to set realistic expectations for your child. It also allows you to help them reach age-appropriate milestones and celebrate them together. Keep in mind, however, that each child has individual differences regarding when and how they develop different skills.

- **Encourage Your Child to Trust Themselves:** Remind your child that all their thoughts and feelings are valid and that they should trust them. This helps foster emotional awareness and intelligence. Taking note of their feelings doesn't mean that you must act on them.

- **Celebrate Positive Moments:** Celebrating positive moments – even if they're seemingly small – reinforces positive behaviors and achievements, helping build emotional resilience. Acknowledging your child's efforts and successes creates a sense of support and validation, and it boosts their confidence and sense of self-worth.

- **Spend Quality Time Together:** Dedicate time every day to spend quality time with your child without distractions. This helps maintain open lines of communication and enhances your child's mental and emotional health.

- **Allow Them to Work through Their Challenges:** Don't rush to help your child navigate challenges before giving them time to figure things out on their own. Giving them enough autonomy helps them develop problem-solving and critical-thinking skills and increases their resilience.

- **Create Healthy Sleep Habits:** Incorporate adequate sleep into your routine. Sufficient sleep, which is around 11 to 14 hours for toddlers, helps them with mental well-being and emotional regulation. Make sure to implement consistent bedtimes and wakeup times and prioritize their sleep schedule to ensure healthy physical, mental, emotional, and social development.

- **Don't Shy Away from Help:** Don't hesitate to reach out to a child development specialist or any other professional if you need additional guidance or emotional support throughout your parenting journey. Asking for help isn't a sign of weakness but proof that you're working toward becoming a better parent.

In this chapter, you've gained a deeper insight into how your parenting style, behaviors, actions, and communication methods impact your child's well-being. By setting boundaries, exhibiting unconditional love, building a strong support network, establishing effective lines of communication, practicing mindfulness, prioritizing self-care, and enhancing resilience, you can create a supportive and healthy environment for your child to grow and develop.

Conclusion

Parenting toddlers is probably the most difficult task in the world. They have started understanding you a little but still don't understand everything. They have begun to express themselves but cannot show all the range of emotions. It's like taking care of a super-intelligent pet who doesn't know it's intelligent yet.

This book has greatly simplified this difficult task; let's wrap up with an even more simplified summary.

We started by exploring and understanding a bit of a child's psychology. The toddler stage (one to three years) brings about many changes in them. They grow physically, and their cognitive and socio-emotional development reaches a new milestone. Remember that every child is different and has a unique perspective of the world.

Your journey toward positive parenting began with the second chapter, where you learned to reflect on the parenting methods absorbed over the years. You may have a specific idea about being a parent (probably based on your own parents), but it may not be right for new-age children. You need to rethink your parenting goals and shift your perspective to embrace the role of a positive parent.

Disciplining in your time may have been harsh, and it made you into the person you are today, but the same techniques won't necessarily work for your little one. Positive disciplining involves being a guide to them instead of using the traditional punishment-based approach.

Then, you learned the transformative power of positive communication. It involves a number of factors, from active listening to positive attention. It is the first step toward building an emotional bond with your child. Your presence in their daily activities is key to establishing trust in your relationship.

In the next chapter, you entered the world of boundaries, like setting rules and explaining the reasons, which provide a sense of security for your toddler, eventually making them more independent. You learned that three main factors form the pillars of positive parenting: patience, consistency, and love.

Despite your positive approach, you may face many challenges in your parenting. It's important to remain calm while tackling those challenges so your toddler can model your behavior. The final pages explored a few additional tips and strategies you can implement to solidify your positive parenting methods.

Key Takeaways

- Look at the world through your toddler's eyes to understand their perspective.

- Adjust your thoughts and feelings accordingly to better implement positive parenting strategies.

- Disciplining your child involves organically instilling essential life skills rather than doling out punishment.

- Consistent boundaries are necessary for toddlers to control their chaotic lives.

Strive to make the best use of the information and principles offered in this book to ensure that your child thrives throughout the different stages of their life, from toddlerhood to adulthood.

If you enjoyed this book, I'd greatly appreciate a review on Amazon because it helps me to create more books that people want. It would mean a lot to hear from you.

To leave a review:

1. Open your camera app.
2. Point your mobile device at the QR code.
3. The review page will appear in your web browser.

_____

Thanks for your support!

Check out another book in the series

References

4 Steps to Emotional Connection With Your Baby and Toddler | Psychology Today. (n.d.). Www.psychologytoday.com. https://www.psychologytoday.com/us/blog/playful-parenting/202302/4-steps-to-emotional-connection-with-your-baby-and-toddler

4 Ways to Calm Toddler Tantrums. (2015, September 22). Focus on the Family. https://www.focusonthefamily.com/parenting/4-ways-to-calm-toddler-tantrums/

A Parent's Guide to Temper Tantrums. (n.d.). Parents. https://www.parents.com/toddlers-preschoolers/discipline/tantrum/a-parents-guide-to-temper-tantrums/

Astral Academy. (2023, January 17). The Benefits of Developing Strong Communication Skills in Kids. Www.linkedin.com. https://www.linkedin.com/pulse/benefits-developing-strong-communication-skills-kids-astralacademy

Big Feelings and Big Behaviors (Tantrums) | GOV.WALES. (n.d.). Www.gov.wales. https://www.gov.wales/parenting-give-it-time/guidance-and-advice/tricky-moments-and-behaviours/tantrums

Blanc, C. (2023, July). Discipline: How and when to set rules and boundaries. Naitreetgrandir.com. https://naitreetgrandir.com/en/step/3-5-years/behaviour/setting-limits-when-should-i-start/

Bly, J. (2015, October 13). Setting Boundaries for Toddlers. Focus on the Family. https://www.focusonthefamily.com/parenting/setting-boundaries-for-toddlers/

Caring for Kids. (2017). Attachment: A connection for life. Www.caringforkids.cps.ca. https://caringforkids.cps.ca/handouts/pregnancy-and-babies/attachment

CDC. (2021a, February 22). Toddlers (1-2 years old). Centers for Disease Control and Prevention. https://www.cdc.gov/ncbddd/childdevelopment/positiveparenting/toddlers.html

CDC. (2021b, February 22). Toddlers (2-3 years old). Centers for Disease Control and Prevention. https://www.cdc.gov/ncbddd/childdevelopment/positiveparenting/toddlers2.html

Chen, F. (2020). Interactive Imagination Supports Toddlers' Emotion Regulation: A Cultural-historical Case Study in a Chinese-American Family. International Research in Early Childhood Education, 21(1). https://files.eric.ed.gov/fulltext/EJ1313339.pdf

Cinelli, E. (2022, November 14). How to Raise Happy, Healthy Toddlers. Verywell Family. https://www.verywellfamily.com/parenting-advice-for-toddlers-289861

Department of Basic Education. (2012). Positive Discipline and Classroom Management Course Reader School Safety Framework.

https://wcedonline.westerncape.gov.za/documents/Psycho-Social%20Support/Positive%20Behaviour%20Programme/PBP%20Resources%20for%20Teachers/positive_classroom_discipline_and_classroom_management_reader.pdf

Discipline: How and When to Set Rules and Boundaries. (n.d.). Naitreetgrandir. https://naitreetgrandir.com/en/step/3-5-years/behaviour/setting-limits-when-should-i-start/

Enns, K. (2017, May 18). 5 Ways To Form Stronger Attachment With Your Children - Crisis & Trauma Resource Institute. Ctrinstitute.com. https://ctrinstitute.com/blog/stronger-attachment-with-children/

Guthrie, G. (2021, January 20). 10 tips for positive communication you can apply today | Nulab. https://nulab.com/learn/collaboration/10-tips-for-positive-communication-you-can-apply-today

Hagan, J., Shaw, J. S., & Duncan, P. M. (2017). Bright Futures: Guidelines for health supervision of infants, children, and adolescents (4th ed.). American Academy of Pediatrics.

How to Stay Calm During Your Toddler's Tantrum, According to a Neuroscientist. (2022, July 21). Lifehacker. https://lifehacker.com/how-to-stay-calm-during-your-toddler-s-tantrum-accordi-1849314522

Jacqueline. (2023, December 26). Proactive Parenting: Preventing Meltdowns, Managing Emotions. Deliberateowl. https://deliberateowl.com/blog/proactive-parenting-preventing-meltdowns-managing-emotions

Lansbury, J. (2012, November 28). Tantrums and Meltdowns - My Secret For Staying Calm When My Kids Aren't. Janet Lansbury. https://www.janetlansbury.com/2012/11/tantrums-and-meltdowns-my-secret-for-staying-calm-when-my-kids-arent/

Johnson, N. (2009, July 21). 16 Limit Setting Tips for Your Toddler or Preschooler. The Baby Sleep Site - Baby / Toddler Sleep Consultants. https://www.babysleepsite.com/toddlers/limit-setting-toddler/

Johnson, N. (2009, July 21). 16 Limit Setting Tips for Your Toddler or Preschooler. The Baby Sleep Site - Baby / Toddler Sleep Consultants. https://www.babysleepsite.com/toddlers/limit-setting-toddler

Lamberg, E. (2020). 11 Effortless Ways to Show Your Child You Love Them. Parents. https://www.parents.com/parenting/better-parenting/simple-ways-to-show-your-child-your-love

LCPC, J. D. (2022, February 10). The Importance of Routines, Schedules and Predictability for Children. JCC Chicago Early Childhood. https://earlychildhood.jccchicago.org/blog/the-importance-of-routines-schedules-and-predictability-for-children/

Learning to Practice Proactive Parenting - STEPS Ministries. (2020, January 10). STEPS. https://lifeimprovementsteps.com/proactive-parenting-toolkit/

Luxton, D. D. (2007). The Effects of Inconsistent Parenting on the Development of Uncertain Self-Esteem and Depression Vulnerability. ResearchGate. https://www.researchgate.net/publication/29444521_The_Effects_of_Inconsistent_Parenting_on_the_Development_of_Uncertain_Self-Esteem_and_Depression_Vulnerability

Marcin, A. (2021, September 24). Why Toddlers Need Routine – and a Sample Schedule to Get You Started. Healthline; Healthline Media. https://www.healthline.com/health/parenting/toddler-schedule#sample-routine

Miller, C. (2016, February 25). How to Handle Tantrums and Meltdowns. Child Mind Institute; Child Mind Institute. https://childmind.org/article/how-to-handle-tantrums-and-meltdowns/

Mindell, J. A., & Williamson, A. A. (2018). Benefits of a bedtime routine in young children: Sleep, development, and beyond. Sleep Medicine Reviews, 40(1), 93–108. https://doi.org/10.1016/j.smrv.2017.10.007

Moline, J. (2022, February 22). Parenting 101: A Brief Reflection on Raising Children. Good Faith Media. https://goodfaithmedia.org/parenting-101-a-brief-reflection-on-raising-children/

Moore, L. (2018, March 6). Want to Be More Patient with Your Kids? Here's How. Psych Central. https://psychcentral.com/blog/tips-for-being-more-patient-with-your-kids#the-larger-picture

Morin, A. (2020, September 28). Positive Reinforcement to Improve a Child's Behavior. Verywell Family. https://www.verywellfamily.com/positive-reinforcement-child-behavior-1094889

Morin, A. (2021, March 27). How to Manage Misbehavior With Discipline Without Punishment. Verywell Family. https://www.verywellfamily.com/the-difference-between-punishment-and-discipline-1095044

Neece, C. L., Green, S. A., & Baker, B. L. (2012). Parenting Stress and Child Behavior Problems: A Transactional Relationship Across Time. American Journal on Intellectual and Developmental Disabilities, 117(1), 48–66. https://doi.org/10.1352/1944-7558-117.1.48

Netra. (2020, November 15). 20+ Reflective Journal Prompts for Positive Parenting. The Brown Perfection. https://thebrownperfection.com/2020/11/15/20-journal-prompts-positive-parenting/

Parent Case Studies. (n.d.). Conscious Parenting. https://happymeparenting.com/parent-case-studies/Parental Stress. (n.d.). University of Minnesota Extension. https://extension.umn.edu/stress-and-change/parental-stress

Parenting Services. (2020, December 23). The power of consistency while parenting young children. Sanford Health News. https://news.sanfordhealth.org/parenting/the-power-of-consistency

Parents. (2015, July 14). 22 Moms Share the Real Joys of Parenthood. Parents; Parents. https://www.parents.com/parenting/better-parenting/the-real-joys-of-being-a-mom/

Planalp, E. M., Nowak, A. L., Tran, D., Lefever, J. B., & Braungart-Rieker, J. M. (2021). Positive Parenting, Parenting Stress, and Child Self-regulation Patterns Differ Across Maternal Demographic Risk. Journal of Family Psychology. https://doi.org/10.1037/fam0000934

Raising Children. (2017, November 2). Temperament: what it is and why it matters. Raising Children Network. https://raisingchildren.net.au/newborns/behaviour/understanding-behaviour/temperament

Relationships with toddlers: ideas and tips. (n.d.). Raising Children Network. https://raisingchildren.net.au/toddlers/connecting-communicating/connecting/connecting-with-your-toddler

Schilling, E. (2018). Temper Tantrums (for Parents) - Nemours KidsHealth. Kidshealth.org. https://kidshealth.org/en/parents/tantrums.html

Setting boundaries for toddlers and preschool children | Family Lives. (2024, March). Www.familylives.org.uk. https://www.familylives.org.uk/advice/early-years-development/behaviour/setting-boundaries-for-toddlers-and-preschool-children

Shelov, S. P. (2014). Caring for Your Baby and Young Child, Birth to Age 5. American Academy Of Pediatrics.

Spalding, D. (2017, October 12). Watching my children become friends is more joyful than I can express. Motherly. https://www.mother.ly/parenting/watching-my-kids-love-each-other-is-my-greatest-joy/

Sriram, R. (2020, June 24). Why Ages 2-7 Matter So Much for Brain Development. Edutopia. https://www.edutopia.org/article/why-ages-2-7-matter-so-much-brain-development/

Taylor, M. (2022, September 29). How to Use Positive Reinforcement on Your Toddler. What to Expect. https://www.whattoexpect.com/toddler-behavior/teaching-positive-reinforcement.aspx

The Toddler Bonding Guide: Solutions for Mothers in Building Positive. (n.d.). Cots and Cuddles. https://www.cotsandcuddles.com/blogs/cotsandcuddles-blogs/the-toddler-bonding-guide-solutions-for-mothers-in-building-positive-connections

Image Sources

1. https://unsplash.com/photos/man-carrying-baby-boy-and-kissing-on-cheek-FqqaJI9OxMI
2. https://www.pexels.com/photo/woman-reading-book-to-toddler-1741231/
3. https://www.pexels.com/photo/girl-in-red-dress-playing-a-wooden-blocks-3662667/
4. https://www.pexels.com/photo/photo-of-family-having-fun-with-soccer-ball-4148842/
5. https://www.pexels.com/photo/a-woman-spending-time-with-her-kids-8084512/
6. https://www.pexels.com/photo/faceless-person-punishing-black-girl-7114747/
7. https://www.pexels.com/photo/african-american-father-with-kids-sitting-near-suitcase-4546014/
8. https://www.pexels.com/photo/kid-wearing-crown-sitting-on-bed-6651865/
9. https://www.pexels.com/photo/photo-of-woman-and-girl-talking-while-lying-on-bed-4473774/
10. https://www.pexels.com/photo/a-happy-family-talking-to-each-other-5792899/
11. https://www.pexels.com/photo/photo-of-a-family-doing-a-therapy-session-7447261/
12. https://www.pexels.com/photo/happy-family-sitting-on-brown-couch-5103909/
13. https://www.pexels.com/photo/a-couple-kissing-their-children-5593100/
14. https://www.pexels.com/photo/blue-jeans-3036405/
15. https://www.pexels.com/photo/photo-of-man-carrying-baby-standing-on-wooden-dock-3933491/
16. https://www.pexels.com/photo/boy-child-playing-outdoors-on-wooden-stairs-5216834/
17. https://www.pexels.com/photo/parents-playing-with-their-children-5103410/
18. https://www.pexels.com/photo/a-family-lying-down-on-the-white-bed-7296217/
19. https://unsplash.com/photos/boy-in-gray-and-white-striped-shirt-sitting-on-floor-WSWHjPGGEY4
20. https://unsplash.com/photos/girl-smiling-while-lying-on-grass-field-at-daytime-ifM0755GnS0
21. https://unsplash.com/photos/woman-sitting-on-white-bed-while-stretching-wBuPCQiweuA

Made in the USA
Monee, IL
11 December 2024

73304801R00052